D1570424

1

Potty Training for Girls in 3 Days

The Step-by-Step Guide to Potty Train and get your Toddler Diaper Free in just a Weekend.

Bonus Chapter with Special Tips and Tricks for your Baby Girl.

AURORA REED

Table of Contents

Introduction

You've picked up this guide for one of two very different reasons: either you've been trying to get your little girl potty trained for a while now and you're ready to tear out your hair with the frustration of it all; or you have yet to give it a go but you've heard some of the horror stories other parents like to share and you'd prefer to make sure none of them happen to you.

Either way, the outcome is going to be the same, of that I can assure you. We're going to get to the bottom of this (no pun intended), one of the trickiest moments in a parent's life, and make sure that it goes as smoothly and accident free as possible.

What we're going to do together is get from zero to potty familiar in the space of just three days. In that short space of time, your tot will be out of diapers, aware of the potty and what it's for and willing to use it when it's time for nature to call. Yes, that's right: just three days. They will be long, tiring days that require your full attention, but that really is as long as it's going to take to get potty training on track and the diapers gathering dust.

Think of it as a boot camp. You're going to make some serious progress with your little girl's development during this time and it's going to happen a lot quicker than you expect.

I want you to know from the start, though, that I can't promise you that your little one will be heading for the potty religiously by the end of day one. I can't promise you that this will be done and dusted by the time the weekend is out, because there is going to be a maintenance period after you're done. In a lot of cases, the techniques we're going to cover will get from square one to the finish line much more quickly than you'd dare hope but bear in mind that every child is different.

Also, some tots have a difficult time with potty training for one reason or another, and that's ok. It doesn't mean it won't happen and it doesn't mean it has to be the most frustrating experience of your collective lives. It just means that there might be a few more days or weeks between introducing youth little girl to this new, personal throne and the moment when you don't need to worry about whether it's getting used.

Potty training gets a lot of bad press. A lot of people think that it's a nightmare because that's what they're told it's going to be. And, sure, it does involve an excess of bodily fluids, occasionally in the kind of places you never wanted to see them land, but the truth is that it's just another milestone in the magical journey of childhood.

It can also be hellishly confusing – which I'm sure you already know, if you've spent some time browsing the internet or the library before landing on these pages. Every parent, every expert and every parenting magazine has a different idea of what you should be doing and why that technique and no other is bound to work. So, which one are you supposed to choose?

The answer to that is: you should choose the one that works best for your little girl, and for you as her parents. As with most things in life, that technique is the simplest of all of them, and is the one we're going to cover.

And so, we're going to walk through the stages of getting your child potty trained together to make sure it's as effortless for all of you as it can possibly be. We'll look at some common problems, including accidents, and what you can do to avoid or solve them. It's as simple as that.

There are also some very clear advantages to getting the potty training stage of your daughter's life out of the way, even if it's not very convenient timing right now or your mother in law is telling you that she is definitely not ready for that sort of thing or everything you read tells you that you should "wait until your baby is ready" before you give it a go.

For a start, just think of the cost that all those diapers are inflicting on your wallet, not to mention the space in your local landfill that they are taking up once they have been used and discarded and the effect that something that's essentially plastic-packaged sewage is having on the environment.

But most importantly is the effect it will have on your child. Though it's not going to be as big a deal to you to get this done and dusted as all those "experts" keep telling you, it's going to be massively influential for your daughter. It's going to establish and build a sense of self esteem from the experience of trying and succeeding to meet a goal and achieve a new skill. It's going to bring her one small step closer to independence and show your toddler that the whole world is waiting for her and she's going to succeed however she chooses to explore it.

So here we go: the three-day potty-training adventure is about to begin. Steel yourself, because this is going to be quite the exciting ride!

Chapter 1 - Why Potty Training for Girls is Very Different for Boys

Being a parent is arguably the best feeling in the world and having your little ones run around in excitement and curiosity is invaluable for most parents. We would want these little ones, however, playing around knowing that they know just what to do when they really 'have to go'. We try to pick up so many tricks and advice that worked for other parents, but we almost fail to consider the fact our children are different, and timing is one of the most important aspects of potty training.

Potty training is slightly different with girls as compared to boys and we shall see why. I believe that little girls are more cautious, and parents should expect them to be more inquisitive.

There is not a lot of information on potty training girls mainly because it is assumed that all children can be potty trained the same. This is not entirely wrong since there are obviously various elements in the training that apply to both girls and boys. Also, I must point out that both parents are completely capable of potty training their little girls if the right tactics are implemented.

The need to potty train your little girl will come naturally since there will be some cues that all parents pick up. This will be the time when everyone would want to give their view on the matter, and I know it is in the parents' nature to try and pick up every bit of information.

It goes without saying that your little girl must be ready before embarking on this very fundamental step in her growth. I have encountered parents that downright gave up, claiming that their child was impossible to train, and I came to find out that it was all just a case of poor timing. But with girls, it is important to note that their training can start from up to 6 months earlier than boys.

So, what exactly should parents explore before the potty-training process? First and foremost, they should ensure that both parties are in the right mindset. Dealing with little girls can be stressful at times to say the least and it is important to deal accordingly with your little girl's emotions as well as your own.

There are times when parents do not know exactly what to do when their child is throwing tantrums, crying and all sorts of things that little girls do. Parents must also understand that the potty-training process will also invoke some not-so-favorable emotions and they must be able to deal with the ugly side of the process. Even though potty training your little girl is possible, there may be times when you would consider other options.

Thus, parents can get frustrated or angry and judging from all the parents I have had the opportunity to interact with I must mention that this is completely normal. Also, your little girl is growing, and she embraces every chance she gets to learn something new. Therefore, it's important that your child is comfortable with the introduction of a new concept by paying close attention to her emotions.

Potty training success is largely measured by the extent to which you and your child will be able to follow the process in a stress-free manner so try to implant the idea that no stress equals success.

Potty training is essentially refining the present bathroom methods to a process that is better controlled by your child. In essence, it is both something new and a refinement of something old and parents must ensure that their child understands this concept before embarking on the training process. If there is any doubt as to whether your little girl is not ready for such a progression, then I suggest a revision of the course of action.

Timing

Pre-training activities rely heavily on the timing in order to implement the best procedure. Most children show signs of potty-training readiness around the age of two, but girls generally train earlier and faster. Therefore, girls can be potty trained around the age of one and a half years. I must stress that you will only potty train your child successfully if she is ready. Any earlier attempts may be unfruitful.

Kids can be very picky and parents that are interested in potty training their children must ensure that their children can easily follow simple commands. One of the most important indicators that your child is ready to be trained is the daily occurrence of bowel movements at the same time. This requires strict observation by parents in order to determine any existing pattern that your little girl may have developed.

Also, training would be a successful project if it results to your child sleeping and waking up dry. This does not only mean during the night but also if she can keep dry for a number of hours during the day. This normally occurs naturally, and your child will continue to stay dry for longer as she grows. Also, children are very observant and if you notice her watching you and asking questions about the toilet then she is ready.

Timing does not only apply to your child but also the whole family as well. It would be very distracting for your little one to potty train when there are other activities taking place. These distractions may occur in various times such as the holidays and other celebrations. Thus, it would be very difficult for any parent to train their child when there is too much going on during Christmas, the hype around Easter etc.

Additionally, potty training is not a spontaneous activity. It should be well-thought through and deciding in the morning that you'll potty train your child in the afternoon will yield little to no results. I suggest creating an action plan at least a few weeks before. This should be done with your child's age in mind.

Helping Your Child

Pre-training largely comprises of the readiness of your child and the parent's role is to be the main guide for whichever activity that will take place. Thus, as a parent, you must ensure that whatever you relay to your child will support them with this transition.

First, parents must ensure that their child is relatively familiar with bathroom terminology. Your child must know about the toilet, the sink, bathroom essentials such as tissues and soaps and their various uses. In order to do so, it is important that your child, accompanied by her siblings and/or her parent, is able to go into the bathroom and understand the activities that take place in that area. Make bathroom trips informative and fun and you will find that your child will slowly pick up more and more information which will help to build their confidence.

There are parents that do not feel comfortable with many people contributing to the training process i.e. the siblings and other female family members. This is totally normal, and I would be better if either mummy or daddy handles the process accordingly.

Also, this is the perfect time to help your little girl determine whether she is wet or not. Teach her to differentiate between the feelings of about to go, being wet and wetting. Make sure she can adequately tell the difference since she needs an active guide.

This step will be easily done by observing her movements and pointing out what is happening when you see her show gestures of being pressed or being generally uncomfortable. Read her movements since every child most likely has her own way of showing that she has to go.

For instance, I know that one of the most common gestures is your child pacing uncomfortably up and down. I've also seen children who squat and hold their crotch area. The point is that the parent must be able to pick up on these cues and help their child understand all these sensations.

Parent Preparation

Potty training would be best executed if possibly both parents are able to contribute. Therefore, the first step in parent preparation is discussion by both parents. The training process will be more successful if your little girl sees both of you wanting the same thing. It will be easier to instruct her as there are children that respond better to either parent or even both which will be an invaluable advantage.

Essentially, parent preparation means that both parents have to be on board and on the same page. I think that discussing every detail is important because it will enable either parent to give the same instructions. As we shall see, naming is a very important aspect of the process and we would not want mummy calling it to pee while daddy calls it something else. This will only confuse your child and make it difficult for her to retain information.

For the parents, being on the same page also means that both of you can comfortably agree on when to start the process. It would be best for your child if both of you agree on a workable schedule. This is meant to avoid scenarios such as the successful start of the process with both parents present and then one having to leave halfway due to circumstances such as business trips etc.

However, this does not necessarily mean that both parents must be there 24/7, watching her as she goes to the bathroom. It will be beneficial if the parents support each other to ensure that their little girl gets the best possible supervision. Ideally, less demanding time such as the weekend would be perfect for spending with your child. Parents must also be mindful if their child has other engagements, such as daycare or play dates, as there is a risk, they could forget what they have been taught.

As mentioned, it is important for your child to recognize the dry and wet sensation thus it is up to the parent to ensure that the differences are clearly understood. For one, I recommend shying away from absorbent diapers as you prepare to potty train your child. Diaper transitioning depends on what you, as a parent, would decide but less absorbent diapers will assist your child in explaining her sensations.

Furthermore, preparation should include extensive data collection. There are so many resources that parents can work with on the Internet and from other parents that have successfully potty trained their child. The best approach is to use the most interactive resources and I think videos can be very helpful. Read up on your child's anatomy, general behavior, other potty-training stories etc. Try and get resources for both you and your child because not only will they assist in the pre-training stage but during the process as well. Fun reading materials and videos with characters will make the process enjoyable for your little girl.

Choosing Your Child's First Potty

You have thought out your plan and made your schedule more flexible for your child's training process. It is now time to choose the most ideal tool of the process. The key is to ensure that your child ends up being comfortable while using the regular toilet which needs an active transition.

Choosing a potty is a significant step in pre-training because you want your child to familiarize herself with this tool that she will use for quite some time. Leave it out before the training begins in order for her to get used to the idea. Teach her what to do with it before she actually uses it in order to find out her general attitude towards it. For now, I would suggest that your young one own only one potty, and as she continues to use it you can purchase another one, with her help of course! With time, you can ensure that every bathroom in the house contains a potty that your child is familiar with and can use comfortably.

Chapter 2 - What Is Potty Training?

The parenting stage of running behind an active toddler can be as fulfilling as it may be exhausting. From first steps to first ball kicking attempts, toddlers need extensive diaper support to take them through their busy days. However, diaper routines are often tedious for mothers and uncomfortable for toddlers. In fact, the very sign of their aging is a constant reminder that they need to be ushered into autonomous habits relatively early in order to best enjoy their lives. After all, there is nothing as challenging as a child stuck in infantile cycles. Whether your child is refusing to sleep through nights or battling the transition to the potty, your approach needs to be the same. You will have to muster both patience and a firm, determined attitude to get the best results from your little one.

Before we dig into the basics of potty training, you will need to assert your objectives as a parent. Ideally, you will discuss this - where need be - with your significant other and vocalize, in all honesty, your hopes for the process. It isn't uncommon for parents to wish to rush the process as much as possible. A busy life, for one, may require you to expedite the process to take one thing off your parent plate. This can result into a classic case of parental guilt, where either or both parents will feel like they are neglecting their child by rushing them through such a crucial transition.

Introduction to Potty Training

Potty training, also known as toilet training, is the process of training a child to seek out the potty for defecation or urination. For the purpose of efficacy, we will focus mostly on the modern approach to potty training.

Little is known about how pre-modern societies dealt with this transition. However, there is reason to believe that centuries ago, toddlers were taught to use toilet facilities mostly through observation. Modern living, however, will require a more controlled, discreet evolution. Furthermore, the toilets of today operate using basic mechanisms that your child will need to learn to enjoy full toilet autonomy. This view of potty training is in line with basic cognitive psychology and behavioral psychology concepts, which we will dig into further after some time.

Naturally, there are many different techniques for potty training, and none of them are wrong. Each child is different;

therefore, every individual child may have relatively individual needs. Every child is also responsive in a different way to parental guidance and other probing stimuli. Some children may struggle more than others to focus on their parents' words. This can make teaching basic concepts relatively difficult. Other children may have fantastic attention spans and will quickly internalize the softest of parental commands as a word of law. Such children will often be easy to potty train using a classic approach. If your child struggles to respond encouragingly during this stage, however, no need to despair. Plenty of alternative, innovative, and effective methods of potty training exist, and we shall discuss in a moment.

It is important to remember, before considering the specifics of each method, that there is little to no evidence of the comparative efficiency of any method. It will be up to you, as a parent, to ascertain, based knowledge of your child's character, the approach which may work best. Therefore, it could be beneficial to begin with either an internal discussion or chat with your significant other about your child. How sensitive are they? How likely are they to venture out on their own? When attempting to teach them a lesson, are they focused on your voice? Do they remember your words? Do they seek your approval? Are they easily alarmed?

As we go deeper into potty training techniques, you will want to have an answer to the questions mentioned above. It is also advised that you choose the technique best suited to your child, as opposed to the one you believe would garner the quickest results.

In western cultures, toilet training usually begins between the ages of 18 months and 2 years old. There is evidence to suggest that babies are capable of being toilet trained earlier. However, the convenience of diapers in the early stages means that there is no point rushing your child into toilet training before 18 months. Furthermore, even children toilet trained relatively early may experience "accidents" well past the age of 4. This suggests that until the age of 5, the average child doesn't possess the capacity to control their bladder or bowel movements entirely. Things such as stress, anxiety, and other strains may often lead a child that has been potty trained into relieving themselves outside of the toilet. This can be a cause of great shame some children may carry with them. Therefore, it is imperative that during the potty training of your toddler, you maintain realistic expectations. This is not an exact science, and your child is often likely to forget herself for a few weeks or even months.

In rare cases, parents may experience particular difficulties potty-training the child, and these may be signs of a physical or behavioral disorder. Such disorders can delay the learning process for the child, which can be incredibly frustrating for the parent(s). If you find yourself frustrated by how slow your child's response is to your training, you may want to call on a professional to intervene. Your pediatrician is best suited to point out such a professional for you. You want to deal with a child psychiatrist or psychologist depending on the severity of the case and your comfort with either approach. Fortunately, you can expect your child to be fully potty-trained regardless of the medical assistance you choose. Some children just take longer than expected. The vast majority, however, can successfully be potty trained by the age of 3.

Toilet training has recently been under scrutiny for its ability to trigger abusive tendencies. The transition to the potty is the time at which your child will feel most vulnerable. They may be confused about the changes they are required to go through. They may even feel frightened by their own inability to make mummy or daddy happy. During that time, parents may feel discouraged and raise their voice. Children may be subjected to punishment, such as not receiving the cleaning they require. This is considered discipline through mild humiliation and is a form of emotional abuse.

If you catch yourself experiencing any of the following during your child's potty training, you may want to contact a professional:

- Irrational anger

- Spite towards your child or spouse

- A desire to inflict punishment

- A desire to create ultimatums

- A desire for abandonment or desertion

While the sentiments listed above can be experienced even without the real urge to harm your child, you may want to examine your urges closely. They can be significant of your own experiences growing up, perhaps the wrath of a parent during that very stage of your life. It isn't infrequent for parents to mimic the attitudes they felt around them at the same age when raising their own toddlers.

This can be beneficial, as it may allow you to sympathize with the child as your subconscious recalls your own emotional reaction to some of these methods. Before you take any disciplinary action during the potty-training stage - whether or not related to the potty itself - you will want to ask yourself how you would have responded in such a vulnerable stage. Children can sense their parents' calm or anxiety. Therefore, remaining the picture of patience - without steering away from the goals you have set with your child - may lead to much more effective toilet training than the use of threats and punishment. If anything, the latter is likely to frighten and confuse your child. This will overwhelm your toddler, who is likely to experience much more incidents, potentially even remain stuck at that stage for a while, as a result.

Why You Need to Potty Train

To put this simply, potty training is crucial due to the presence of toilets in our daily lives.

The oldest modern toilet is deemed to date back to Ancient Rome. However, it took centuries for the "specialized lavatories" to become a common sight in affluent households. As far as researchers have been able to ascertain, modern toilets were deemed inconvenient because of the lack of sanitation equipment and techniques in ancient societies.

Similarly, the concept of wrapping children into linen to prevent the spreading of sudden releases is relatively modern. However, fecal matter has often been linked to the spreading of diseases; therefore, it was merely a matter of time before nappies were invented. One can deduce that this may have brought on the first instance of potty training, as parents attempted to make the transition from cloth nappies, they had to hand wash to the use of the equipment existent in the 1800's.

As societies modernized, the family structure shrunk, and women were granted more work opportunities. Unfortunately, in the 20th century, this involved a double burden for the woman, who was required both to tend to the home and the upbringing of the children. This desire for emancipation from the more unpleasant and strenuous tasks in the home led to the ascension of disposable diapers to the top of baby-caring norms. This change was simultaneous with the arrival of washing machines in the western market, which alleviated the burdens of home care.

Women were then able to spend more time at work or tending to activities other than childcare at home. They were encouraged to gain autonomy in order to maintain active lives, well into motherhood. This meant that children had to be trained to act autonomously as early as possible, preferably to avoid incidents now considered out of the ordinary. A certain stigma was placed on children late to use the toilet or still prone to spoiling themselves. This stigma walks hand in hand with the "parent-blaming," which may result from another adult witnessing such an incident. This led to a certain stress being put on the parent to overcome the dirty, unpleasant stage of diapers as quickly as possible.

Naturally, this stress isn't entirely unhealthy. After all, a certain amount of pressure is necessary for the parents to fully grasp the inconvenience of diapers to a growing toddler's life.

Most toddlers are walking comfortably by the 18 months and running around at a marvelous speed by the age of 2. At this point, they are old enough to grasp the societal implications of having soiled pants, but not what is expected from them in return. They will be sensitive to unpleasant smells, which they will associate with shaming and may feel uncomfortable carrying around. Besides, the wet material may feel uncomfortable against their skin or even cause rashes. This will heavily disturb their most rewarding developmental activities (running around/playing with friends/taking a walk with either or both parents, etc.), which may cause anxiety and even anger in your child.

To avoid a fixation on this stage, you may want to address the issue early on.

You should also note that some activities may simply not be available to your child until they are potty-trained. Kindergarten and most daycare centers, for example, can only admit children who can use the toilet. Essentially, leaving your child untrained to use a toilet is freezing them into a state of "babyhood," which may hinder their development.

You may struggle to take a child old enough to be active (to demand to be allowed to walk/run around the store/engage with other children) anywhere unless they are potty trained. This can lead to a classic case of parent guilt and self-imposed isolation.

Chapter 3 - What to Prepare before the 3-Day Potty Training?

If potty training occurs between 9-15 months, take it as an adventurous challenge, rather than a daunting task at hand. When you decide that it's time to potty train your child, the first thing you need to do is to train your patience. Focus on your child and on the training itself.

Preparing the area and Equipment

Choose an area of the house where you will potty train your child. This may be your bathroom, living room or the kitchen.

When it comes to equipment, get a potty or a seat that you put on top of a regular toilet seat. The first option is more common and is a great way to introduce the toilet by presenting a smaller, less intimidating version of it. Some potty seats can come in many different colors and are customizable. You may want to let your child decorate it with stickers or drawings so that she is comfortable in its presence. This will be a good companion of your child so make sure she gets acquainted with it.

The second option allows for a more gradual transition. At this age, children will be so eager to please and take part, so there should be little resistance to toilet use. Make sure there is a little footrest with the seat for your child to use. A sturdy stool on the side can also help, especially when your child doesn't have the coordination to climb up and down the seat yet. Encourage independence but be there to guide your child.

Other equipment and things you may want to consider are a timer, clean underpants, your child's favorite toys and games, sketchpads, crayons, coloring worksheets, a waterproof mattress pad, and stickers. Tell your kid that using the potty like a grown-up is an important part of life and make it a reason to celebrate.

Feeding for Success

Choosing the right area and potty is one thing, but since potty training is all about elimination, you can make the experience easier by helping your child eat the right food. Amp up the likelihood of your child being in a frame of mind of eliminating by increasing fiber and water intake. Here are some stool-softening foods you can try out: peaches, pear nectar, apricots, berries, plums, prune juice, grapes, vegetables, or apple juice.

Try to stay away from food that tends to constipate or harden stool such as white bread, cheese, excessive milk, or pasta.

The Plan

Once everything is ready to go, it is now time to prime up your child's mindset. You can tell her that you will be organizing a potty party for her and that all her toys will be attending. Explain the importance of doing the training and that it is an important part of her being a big girl and growing up. You can try to show her colorful underwear and ask her to try it on. Some parents recommend that during potty training, the child should stay naked from the waist down. But this is unnecessary, and you can do without this step.

For the first few weeks, start the day with a visit to the potty as soon as she wakes up. Make this a daily morning ritual. Walk to her room, pull up the curtains, throw her a big good morning kiss, then declare, "It's time to wake up and go to the toilet." This way, you are not asking your child's opinion, but stating it as a fact of life. By leaving out her choice, you are making the act as normal as telling her it's time to brush her teeth. Do not ask, just do it.

He may have peed during the night, so the diaper may still be wet, and she may not want to pee again. Sit her in the potty for no more than 5 minutes. Hold her hand and get comfortable by telling a story, singing a song, or talking about her day ahead. Make it a pleasant experience each time. If she does urinate, associate it with yourself by saying, "Oh look, you're peeing the way Mommy does. That's great!" Children at this age want to imitate Mom and Dad. This will give her the encouragement she needs. Once she is done, show your child how to wipe herself clean. This is the same for both genders, whether it's peeing or pooping. Little girls should be taught to wipe front to back. They may struggle and not get it right immediately, so be prepared to have all hands-on deck. You might have to do it yourself. But if you do, talk your child through what you are doing. Make sure they understand the importance of cleaning up after themselves.

If your child is unable to pee, take her off the potty. Put on a new diaper and give her breakfast. Around 20 minutes after your child drinks liquids, put her on the potty again and repeat the process. Do this for the rest of the day, after she drinks or when you think she will have another bowel movement again. Some children pee or poo right before a bath. If this applies to your child, take the opportunity to toilet train her again.

For the first few weeks, go slowly but remain consistent. Try to avoid placing your child on the potty for only once a day. This can be confusing for the child, who may end up thinking that the potty is only used after breakfast or before taking a bath. Help your child develop her senses by keeping her in touch with her bodily functions and sensations. Make her see the connection between elimination and sitting on the toilet or potty. She may still have incomplete control over her sphincter muscles. Provide her with the opportunity to recognize these sensations and practice control. This will make the transition as smooth as possible.

Always remember that your child will learn everything within a week or two. It's a common myth to "learn potty training in 3 days." Do not give up or feel frustrated when it seems to take longer than you expect. The more supportive you are, the more likely your child will want to succeed.

Establishing the Steps

When giving verbal instructions, keep in mind that you have to go as slow as you possibly can. Allow your child to take in the information, and carefully explain each step from sitting down to flushing.

A child learns best when being shown what to do, so you may tell him, "Watch how I pull down my pants. Now, let's see you try it. Then let's see you climb on the potty, just to see how fun it is!" For the child to feel like a self-starter, that's a good thing.

Then, talk about how when one sits on the potty, that's where your poop or pee goes. You may use examples of her older sisters, or the toilet for mommy and daddy. Explain to her in an enthusiastic way how toddlers like her are moving up to training pants to use the potty and that it is such an important milestone in a growing little girl.

Afterwards, show your child how to wipe herself clean. You may hold off teaching her this step once she has fully learned how to eliminate inside the potty. There is no rush but show her that it is important to clean herself up after she does her business. Once she moves on to toilet training, you can then teach her to flush. Try to make it fun, but explain to her that toilets aren't toys, and these are the types of bathroom equipment one shouldn't play with. If your child voices out concern about falling inside the toilet, tell her that it may be big enough to hold her poop and toilet paper, but not large enough to swallow her whole. Do not bore her with detailed explanations on plumbing – just keep it light and fun in terms she will understand. When it comes to diaper disposal, talk to her about how her toys all belong in a particular box or space and that her poop should have a designated place for it as well. Your child may react to this in many different ways. Some may be interested or even fascinated by the idea, and some may feel scared or anxious about the sudden disappearing act. Take your cue on how to respond by listening and watching for her reactions to this step.

This will help you learn to readjust your training accordingly. Also, avoid shaming her by making statements like, "Your poop is really stinky today" or "You really dirtied your diaper." These statements will make your child feel as though she has done something naughty and is a cause for embarrassment. It does not help with the potty-training process as she will interpret going to the toilet as an act of shame instead. Don't make her feel funny about dropping her poop and pee in hollow spaces.

Lastly, show her how to wash up her hands by singing the Happy Birthday song while her hands are being lathered with warm water and soap. Teach her that learning to use the potty is only as successful as knowing how to keep herself clean afterward.

Potty Training for Girls

Girls are usually potty-trained earlier than boys. Girls tend to be more particular about hygiene than boys. As with regular potty training, allow her to sit on the potty first. Teach your little girl how to wipe the right way from the front to the back. This prevents bringing germs from the anal region to the vaginal opening, which can lead to urinary tract infections. Keep in mind that if girls wear diapers for far too long, it can increase the risk of developing a bladder infection. Entice her with underwear that is brightly colored with cute designs. Allow her to choose the design she wants so that she will feel more responsible and more adult-like. This will encourage her to use the potty more to wear cute underwear.

Chapter 4 - How to Potty Train a Child in 3 Days

As you are tucking your child in for the night, tell them that tomorrow is a very important day. Tomorrow they will begin using the potty! Make it sound fun and exciting. Let them know that if they use the potty they will be rewarded. Let them know that they will be given real underwear to wear and show it to them. Even if they helped you pick it out, remind them of it and show them again. Make sure they know that tomorrow is an important day, and they should get some rest to make the most of it.

Arrange that nobody is home on the morning of your practice day. Please note on both the door that you don't want disruptions, turn your answering machine on, and shut off your mobile phone. For just the rest of each day, you'll give your baby all your publicity and obey the toilet training plan guidance. Teach your kids first to tell the doll we have to go to the potty chair. It gives your little girl a sense of why and how to go to the bathroom. They should learn how to take the potty in time, take down their pants, wait for the pot to urinate, pull-up their pants, then empty the pan (with false urine) and then put it back into the potty chair. The child must also clearly complement the doll and encourage it when the toy goes to the potty chair and wees.

Give them plenty of drinks here so they can go to the bathroom in abundance. Tell them one step at a time how to quickly get their pants down (it is beneficial to have two sizes too big), how to sit on her toilet, and relax until they urinate or have a bowel movement. Then, how to clean it, pull it up and drain the pot into the bath, and put it back in the potted seat.

Your child should receive awards for her correct conduct and learning. Then let the child know what to do when they have an accident, how to go to the toilet when they play, how to get to the bathroom when they play outside. They can receive rewards and praise for their dry pants.

They don't have to wear diapers in bed that night. Leave a light on at night, and you can place the potty chair beside their bunk. The following day you can celebrate with your child and give them a completion certificate for toilet training. Yes, it can happen, and in just one day, your child can be trained in the toilet!

If you have a kid, most likely, you were asked the standard question, "Is your little child potty trained yet?" Your reply is still more likely to be no! Ultimately it will not be possible to learn the toilet until your child is ready. This usually happens when a child is between 18 and 24 months old. It is not uncommon, however, for a child still to be two and a half to 3 years old in diapers.

Several other factors are more important than your child's age: can they stay dry at least three hours a day? Can they understand simple instructions and follow them? Are they interested in "big-girl" activities like brushing their teeth, cleaning up their toys, and using the toilet? If so, they might be prepared.

You need the strength, stamina, and time to participate in this critical adventure. After the initial planning and to begin this process officially, you have to devote three to five days of intensive training to your child and their toilet. After the first learning phase, you will need another two to three months of continuous effort.

Day 1

As soon as your child gets out of bed for the day put them in a pair of underwear. Take them immediately to the potty and let them try to go. If they don't, give them plenty of praise and act excited about the effort.

If your child has been on a routine schedule and typically goes to the bathroom at the same times of the day, it will be much easier to know when to send them to the potty. When it is about that time become very excited. Through your preparation, your child should also know what it feels like to need to go potty. However, this may not be evident on the first day. They may be shy about going to the potty or think they can wait because they don't realize how quickly the feeling of needing to go turns into going. However, any time your child thinks they need to go potty, get excited and go with them.

Any time your child gets on the potty but doesn't go, be positive. Help them stay excited about the prospect of using the potty. They must not lose this optimism and become frustrated. You should also remain calm and positive, and not get frustrated, even if your child makes messes for you to clean up. Your child will sense your frustration, and it will ruin the entire process.

Ask them if they know that this is where they are supposed to go potty. They will probably tell you yes. If they go even a little bit more, as they might if they stopped going as soon as they realized what was happening, praise them even though they didn't quite make it in time. Send them off to play while you clean up the mess so that they don't realize the hassle they have caused you.

If your child goes potty on their own or with your insistence, you should praise them continually and be very excited. You might come up with a cheer or a song to sing whenever your child goes potty. You might even do a little dance. Whatever gets them excited about the fact that they have gone potty.

You should not give your child a treat or physical reward when they go potty. If you do this right off the bat, they will continue to expect it even after they should be potty trained. They could refuse to go to the potty if you aren't giving them treats anymore. Giving your child treats for going potty is the same as bribing them. It may work for the short term, but long term it spells disaster.

At the end of the day, put your child in a pull-up and tell them that you want to make sure they sleep well so that they can do it again tomorrow. Go over the day's successes and tell them that you are proud of them for their efforts. Let them know that tomorrow will be even better, and stay excited as you tuck them in.

Day 2

Once again, as soon as your child gets up, put their underwear on and take them to the potty. Knowing that they will be going to the potty right away, they may hold it when they first wake up so that they can go in the potty and feel that sense of accomplishment. This is a very good sign.

Today you should make sure that your child is pulling their own underwear up and down. You should also teach them how to wipe themselves with the toilet paper or flushable wipes. Let them try to become more independent today. While you should still suggest the potty frequently, don't take them into the bathroom unless they instigate it, or you can tell that they are about to go. This will help them associate that feeling with the need to go potty and get used to how long they have between that feeling and the actual event.

Continue being excited for your child. Help them stay positive and excited about using the potty. This will help keep them on track. It is much easier for a toddler to remember what they are supposed to be doing and keep from getting sidetracked if they are excited about it.

Day 3

Today is the day your child will be potty trained. This morning tells your child to take off their pull-up and go potty. Do not go in with them. Let them do it on their own. When they have gone, they will be excited and run out to tell you. That is your chance to be excited with them.

Today your child will know when they have to go potty. They will not try to hold it but will go immediately as soon as they know they need to go. They will probably tell you something like "Hey, Mommy! Time to go potty!" and run into the bathroom expecting you to trail after. Follow your child, but don't enter the bathroom. Stand in the doorway and let them feel the independence of using the potty on their own.

Today your child will likely have not a single accident. Even if they have one or two accidents, take it all in stride. Even potty-trained children get sidetracked, engrossed in play or a television show, and forget to go potty. Accidents happen. As long as there are no more than two accidents during the day, and the reasons for them are obvious, do not take this as a bad sign.

By the end of the day, your child will be going potty like a pro. They will not need your help, and they might not even want your help. They might tell you to go away, that they are going potty. You must give them this independence. It is the driving force that will make them keep using the potty and take pride in their ability to do it.

By the end of this day, you can be confident that your child is out of pull-ups forever. You may still want to use a pull-up for a couple of weeks at night until your child gets used to waking up to go to the potty. This can take longer than the three days to mostly potty train your child, and some children with physical problems will need nighttime pull-ups for as long as another year.

When you and the child were ready, it's time to start training potty. But once you start, you can't go back. Tell your child that the diapers are for babies and that she or they are no longer an infant. Go to the store and let your child select new underwear for a "big kid." Let your child throw away a few of their old diapers when you get home and help her put on her underwear. Your child will wear underwear from now on.

Don't hurry them to the pot rapidly if your kid will have an accident. You want to warn them not to go after a crash. Try not to change them directly into dry clothes. They must experience the uncomfortable moisture when they wet themselves. This is a method of training that can take a few days. You should probably stay home for the first few days, but I encourage you to go on a little trip, so your child feels comfortable wearing underwear. For example, the car seat straps need to be changed, and a public toilet is used for a completely different experience.

Place the child on the pot every 10 minutes. DO NOT ASK foolish questions like "You gotta go potty sweet pie!?," we're talking here to a two-year-old! Just do it as it is, don't ask for permission. Don't push it, and just let your little girl decide whether she needs to get up immediately. Set a timeout every 10 minutes if you have a resistant baby. It is remarkable what a kid will do when the power dynamic is withdrawn. It is time to sit on a pot when the "potty timer" goes off.

Chapter 5 - What are Some Potty-Training Tips for Ultimate Success?

Tip #1: Start Talking About the Potty As Early As Possible

Start potty discussions early. As soon as your child starts becoming curious about the potty start discussing it, talk about what it is for, show them what happens if you flush a few cheerios down. Talk about how they will be able to use it and not wear diapers any longer. When you will do this, all depends on the maturity and age of your child. As I said earlier my daughter was potty trained at the age of one, this is not the norm. She was and is a curious child as well as very mature. Start out slow and let your child guide you.

Tip #2: Know That Every Child Will Require Their Own Potty-Training Technique

The second tip I want to give you is that not every technique is going to work on every child. Now don't get me wrong, the three-day intensive potty-training session will work on every child if they are willing to do it. There are going to be some kids who just say no. In addition, you are going to find that no matter what you try to reward them with they are simply going to refuse to even try. This happens when children reach the ages of two or three and begin to realize that they are their own person.

Tip #3: Don't Over Reward Your Child

You may also find that the child is trying to get you to up the ante. For example, if you are offering a candy kiss for using the potty they may refuse, knowing you will offer then two. They can continue this knowing you will always offer more. If you find that, your child is displaying this type of behavior when it comes to potty training, try a little bit of reverse psychology on them.

When I was potty training my youngest, she was getting close to starting preschool. I had many discussions with my mother about her not being able to start because she refused to be potty trained. (She was the baby and wanted to stay that way) So one day I told her I didn't care if she didn't want to be potty trained because if she went to school like her brother and sister I would be alone all day and miss her. When she realized that she could not be a big kid and go to school if she did not use the potty, her attitude changed, and she was ready to start training.

Tip #4: Make Sure Your Child Knows They Will Not Get In Trouble For Soiling Themselves

What about children who hide soiled underpants? I also went through this with my oldest child. She did not want me to know when she had an accident so instead of coming to me she simply hid her spoiled underpants under her bed. Many parents will just clean up the mess, was or discard the soiled underwear and move on trying to save their child the embarrassment of an accident but you need to explain to the child that this is unacceptable.

Talk to the child explaining that they will not be in trouble if they have an accident. Do not scold the child but explain that it is not okay for them to hide soiled underpants. Tell them an accident is okay and you will not be angry with them. Once they understand that you will not be disappointed in them this usually stops. If on the other hand it does not, you may need to go back to diapers for a few months until your child is mature enough to wear underwear.

Tip #5: Let Your Child Use the Potty Wherever They Are The Most Comfortable

You may also find that your child only wants to use the potty at home. If this is the case, you can help them to feel comfortable in public bathrooms before they go. Sometimes children like to explore the public bathrooms, see how the sinks work and how the toilets flush. For those loud self-flushing toilets, make sure you take a pad of sticky notes with you because the shock of the toilet flushing on its own can frighten some kids causing them to regress when it comes to toilet training. You can also "demonstrate" how the public toilets work for your child. Often once they see a parent use it, they are fine.

Tip #6: Be Prepared for A Potty-Training Shakeup

Sometimes children will do excellent with potty training and then all of a sudden, they don't. This is usually caused because of a shakeup in their routine. Routine gives a child a sense of security, if they lose that sense of security, they will revert back to things that are more comfortable for them. This is not a failure on your part, you have to understand that setbacks are normal, and we cannot always keep our routines the same. If you find that this is happening with your child, make sure that when your routine is disrupted you are asking the child frequently if they need to use the bathroom. You can even set the timer on your cell phone to help you remember to ask.

Tip: #7: What to Do If You Have A Stubborn Child

There are also children who will only poo in a diaper. They go all day peeing in the potty and as soon as their nighttime diaper goes on, they fill it up. The majority of the time you will find that constipation is to blame for this. If the child was constipated the last time they tried to poo on the potty, they will associate the potty with it hurting when they went poo. Therefore, they will use the diaper because it feels safer to them. The way to handle this is to load the child's diet with high fiber food, which will make it easier for your little girl to poo. If this does not work, you may want to talk to your doctor because some children need a gentle laxative when they are potty training.

Tip #8: Get All Those Involved In Your Child's Life On Board With Potty Training

If your child goes to a sitter or daycare, make sure you get the caretaker on board when it comes to potty training. So many times, I have seen parents working so hard to potty train only to have a caretaker who puts the child in diapers the entire day. This will never work and only confuses the child. If the caretaker refuses to help with potty training, it may be time to start looking for a new one.

Tip #9: Begin Potty Training When You and Your Child Are Ready For It

You can begin very young when it comes to potty training. If you want to start your child off easily, purchase a potty seat and sit it in the bathroom. This is something I did with my daughter. When I had to use the bathroom of course, she would follow me, and I would ask her if she wanted to sit on her potty if she did great if she didn't fine. This got her used to the idea of using the potty at a very early age and as I said before she was potty trained at the age of one.

Tip #10: Buy Underpants That Your Child Will Love

Another tip that really helps with younger children is to purchase underpants with their favorite characters on them. This was one of the tricks I used with my oldest daughter. When she was younger, she was in love with Blue from the show Blues Clues so I went out and bought a ton of Blues Clues themed underpants and gave them to her. Every morning she would put them on and I would tell her remember not to go potty on Blue. This worked wonderfully. Throughout the day I would remind her not to go on Blue and she would say oh no she wouldn't like that. I would also ask her if Blue was still dry and she would smile with pride when she answered yes.

Tip #11: Never Give Up

Don't give up. Remember every child will be ready to potty train at some point. We never hear of anyone graduating from high school still in diapers so don't feel like it is never going to happen. Keep at it and remember you will make it through this. Determination is key. I would love to say that my daughter was so wonderful and easy to train because she is one of those gifted kids but the fact is that when I found out I was pregnant with my third child on my daughters first birthday I absolutely refused to have two in diapers. If you are not determined, it is never going to work.

Tip #12: Brace Yourself for Accidents

Be prepared for accidents. Make sure you are stocked up on carpet cleaners and upholstery cleaners. Being prepared and understanding that accidents are going to happen is going to make it much less stressful when they do happen.

Tip #13: Just Do It!

Just go for it! If you think that your child is ready to be potty trained, grab that big kid underwear and just go for it! The worst that is going to happen is you are going to realize you need to wait a few more months. At best, you are going to be diaper free and that is what we all want!

Tip #14 Learn the Difference of Potty-Training Girls and Boys

Boys and girls are different in many aspects of child rearing, potty training included. One myth is that girls are easier to potty train than boys. This stems from the fact that moms are mostly responsible for potty training. Therefore, girls look up to mommy and want to be just like her. Mom can model proper potty usage for girls, but not for boys. The simple solution is to involve dads or older male figures when potty training boys.

Children tend to think potty dances and songs are much sillier coming from dads, so this is added encouragement for both genders. Also, dads should be thrilled about potty training since it means that they can now take their little buddy out without worrying about lugging a diaper bag.

A tried and true method for boys is putting an object in the toilet and letting them try to "sink" it with pee. Boys also tend to be fascinated with the swirling action of the potty flushing. Girls are more motivated by the prospect of new underwear. Typically, boys are older before they are ready to potty train but catch on quicker. Girls can start a little younger, but peeing takes more effort for them, so it may take a little longer for them to get the hang of it.

Chapter 6 - What are Some Problems Experienced by Parents While Potty Training?

In practice, many children face certain difficulties, mainly because of the following reasons:

- They start toilet training at an early age

- They start the training a little late

- They show signs of "toilet training resistance"

- The parents improperly handle them at the training stage

- There may be some medical/physical reasons

Let's look at each of these reasons one after the other.

Toilet-training at an early age

Early toilet training may lead to day-wetting and constipation. Unrestricted voidance in the diaper by young children who are not ready for toilet training is usually considered beneficial for the normal growth and expansion of the bladder. If, on the other hand, they start training before their bodies are ready, the children may tend to hold back urine and stools for longer periods which is detrimental to bladder growth. According to a research conducted by the Wake Forest Baptist Medical Center starting potty training too early, before the age of 2, could cause day-time wetting problems at a future stage. Also, because the stool is retained for longer periods, these children are prone to constipation.

Besides, it may lead to frustrations, negative attitude and other psychological repercussions.

Hence, it is wiser not to pressure a child into the potty-training process before the child is ready to handle it. This is something that parents can and should discuss with their pediatrician.

Starting potty-training late

Delaying training to an older age (past 36 months) can also be equally detrimental. It could lead to problems like constipation.

In addition, the child may also refuse to go to the bathroom since the child wasn't trained in due time.

Children showing "toilet training resistance"

Some children, who seem to be physically and physiologically ready to be potty-trained, categorically refuse all of their parents' attempts to train them.

If a child of 3 years of age or more, whom the parents have been trying to train for quite some time, refuses to use the potty or toilets for unknown reasons, then such child can be considered as a child who is training resistant.

There are children, who, even if placed over the potty or a toilet, will not go and they will prefer to soil their diapers right after getting off the potty!! This can be very frustrating for parents. Other children, instead, end up soiling themselves, holding back on bowel movement, leading to constipation.

There may be many various reasons explaining this kind of behavior. The child may be stubborn, strong-willed, disinterested or simply afraid of the toilet. In some cases, the resistance exhibited may even be a form of revolt against parental insistence.

So, what can the parents do to overcome this situation?

- Stop reminding the child to use the potty. These children do not want to follow the (direct) instructions of their parents, so a strategy can consist in indirectly encouraging the child to use the toilet to give the child a sense of achieving success on her own. It works wonders.

- Since the child is already mature enough to understand most oral instructions, the parents should make it clear that using the potty, not soiling underpants and maintaining cleanliness by disposing of the waste at the proper place is the child's own responsibility.

- Stop using diapers and training pants or use them less. It will push the child to visit the toilets when needed because at this age the child will be mature enough to understand that soiled underwear is not comfortable.

- When a child not only refuses to use the toilets but also tries to stop the urge for bowel movements, it might lead to constipation and to other medical problems. To avoid this, parents should sit with the child and explain to their child or daughter why it's a good thing to eliminate. There are many reading sources and DVDs designed to explain the potty-training process to a very young audience. Parents can use one of these sources or video programs as an educational tool.

- Choose a toy, a game, a doll or even a cartoon that the child truly likes and use them as an incentive when the child uses the potty properly. The allowance is for a limited time only and under the control of the parent so that the child appreciates the importance of the incentive.

- Make it a point to document the achievements on a chart and show the same to the family physician at the time of visit and praise the child for the improvement. A praise or encouragement in the presence of an authority figure such as the family physician gives good impetus to the child to stick to good habits.

- Some children might resist potty training due to phobias. It's a classic. Some children are afraid that they may fall into the toilet. In such a case, it would be advisable to use a small stool or a box to sit the child more comfortably and to feel confident. If you use a box, make sure that it is safe and that the child cannot fall from it when leaving the toilets and fall into it. Alternately, a potty can be used until such time that the child starts feeling confident enough to use the toilets. Conversely, if the child does not like a potty, the parents can encourage the child to directly use the toilet at home. The comfort of the child is really important.

Improper handling of the children by the parents

Whatever method the parents want to adopt to potty-train their child, there are certain things to do and certain things that should not to be done if they want a smooth transition.

Some things to do:

Pay close attention to the maturity of your child and to the various milestones achieved to decide if this is the right time and then start potty-training. This can be communicated with your pediatrician. You do not necessarily have to make that decision on your own.

This happens to be the most important step in toilet training a child since many aspects of mental maturation, physical readiness, willingness etc. contribute to success or failure of the toilet training exercise.

Choose a potty that the child likes or let the child use the toilet if this is its choice. Make the potty or toilet a pleasant place to be because the child should feel comfortable and stress-free when visiting it.

Choose the time the child is likely to use the potty and lead it to the potty. This is only a temporary phase. The ultimate goal is to get the child to go to the toilet by herself.

The transition from wearing diapers to training pants should be explained to the child by putting this into perspective. Of course, we are talking about a young child but with the proper words this can be easily achieved. The idea it to make her understand the importance of the leap she is making, which in turn, will encourage her to take pride in the achievement instead of treating it as a compulsory hurdle to be crossed.

Praises and incentives must be a part of the training process to make it a pleasurable journey for the child.

What are the "No No's"?

The first, and the most important of all, is that you should not compel the child to train, under any circumstances. It could foster rebellion and ultimately make things more complicated than they should be.

Accidents and regression after the toilet training is completed are quite common. The parents should not show their disappointment or their frustration because it could reflect on the child's behavior.

Some children will not adjust easily and smoothly to toilet training. They may also take a long time to train, much to the frustration of the parents. Again, at no time should the child witness your frustration.

The child should never be punished for lack of improvement, resistance, accidents, regression, etc.

Do not make the child sit on the potty for a long stretch of time, waiting that whatever should happen happens. This will likely result in rebellion.

Do not restrict the child's physical activities as a method of punishment because it will, in fact, have an adverse impact on proper avoidance. Physical activity helps in maintaining your child's good health and well-being, which is a key factor in good bowel movement.

Medical Problems

In some cases, medical problems can interfere with the potty-training. These should always be brought to the attention of your pediatrician. Two conditions in particular can play a role in the difficulty of the training.

Encopresis

Encopresis is the term used when a child repeatedly passes feces at improper places. The main reason for encopresis is chronic constipation, which can come from stress, from fiber deficiency, from the fact that the child does not drink enough water, or from some medical reason such as a sore near the anus etc.

This should be communicated with your pediatrician and one of the solutions usually involves a diet or a change in toilet habits to enable the child to pass stools easily and fully.

If the cause of the problem is the child's anxiety the parents will need to provide a stress-free atmosphere and environment. In some cases, psychotherapy may also be recommended.

Enuresis

Enuresis is a form of incontinence. Basically, the child cannot control when she pees. Most of the time, problems happen during bedtime, but the child may also have daytime wetting accidents. Neither daytime nor bedtime wetting are voluntary for the child, and hence it should be made very clear to the child that she should not feel guilty because it is not the child's fault.

When Should the Parents Seek Help?

As we said, how long it takes to become potty-trained is going to depend on many different factors. It can take very little time, or it can take more efforts. Because it takes more time than the parents imagine it should does not mean that there is anything wrong. Parents should not feel frustrated by delays, regressions, potty accidents or even bed-wetting etc. It can happen, and chances are that it happened to them as well when they were toddlers. They should persevere patiently to obtain positive results.

However, if by the age of 3 the child is not able to adjust to the routine and they have been working on it for quite some time, or it appears that the child might have some medical problem like constipation or diarrhea, they should consider obtaining expert advice.

Potty-training is also a question that can be raised any time the parents bring their child to the doctor, even if it's for a routine visit or at the occasion of vaccinations and normal check-ups. What many parents ignore is that often they can just call their doctor and discuss the issue, or any other issues they may be experiencing, over the phone rather than going to visit the doctor's office, which may sometimes be difficult when both parents are working.

Chapter 7 - What Should Parents NOT Do During the 3-Day Potty Training

Do Not Let Your Child Watch Tv Or Play on The iPad.

This might be a hard rule to follow, but every parent knows when children sit in front of the TV or an electronic device, they turn into little zombies. How many times do you have to say her name before your child responds to you? Zoning out usually means having an accident. A few successful pees in the potty do not make her an expert or mean the new procedures have been reinforced enough that peeing on the potty is now a habit. Kids forget because their conscious minds are basically turned off when the TV is turned on. If watching TV and playing with the iPad are a must for your child, then place her on a towel, sit beside her, and remind her every minute to tell you when she has to go to the bathroom.

Do Not Stare at Your Phone for Longer Than 15 To 30 Seconds.

Remember when I said your kids know how to manipulate you? Well, I promise they will have their pee accidents the exact second you are not paying attention or have left the room. The times when your child has to go pee are the only learning opportunities. If you miss those opportunities because you were playing Candy Crush, you'll have to pump your child full of fluids again, then wait until the time she has to go to the bathroom again. Bummer.

Do Not Leave Your Child Alone in A Room.

Once you put your child into underwear on Day 1 of training, you will be glued to your child until she goes to sleep—whether that's naptime or bedtime. If you go to the kitchen to get lunch,

Little Amy is coming with you. If you have to go to the bathroom, Little Amy is coming, too. If you go to your room to change clothes because you got peed on, Little Amy comes along. If you have to put a load of pee underwear in the washer, Little Amy? Yes, she comes, too. Do you see the pattern? You have to be right there to catch every single accident your child has, or this won't work.

Do Not Give Back Your Child's Diapers.

If you give back your child's diapers because she demands them or throws a fit, you not only show your child she has complete power, but you also set yourself up to fail when you decide to potty train for real in the future. If you give the diapers back once, your child will expect them back every time and will not take you seriously when you say it's time to ditch the diapers. Usually a power struggle will ensue, and your child will throw the tantrum of a lifetime.

Two examples come to mind here, both with girls who had tried potty training in the past, but for which the parents reacted differently in each situation. One mom, a psychologist, wanted to bargain with her child during her screaming fit about wanting diapers back. She refused to put underwear on her daughter or continue potty training until they could talk it through thoroughly. The other mom was a stay-at-home mom who, during her daughter's tantrum (because the child didn't want to put underwear on and wanted her diaper), somehow managed to get the underwear on the screaming girl. Only one of these little girls ended up potty trained. I will let you guess which one. (Okay, I'll tell you! The psychologist's daughter got her diapers back, and it took another six months to get her potty trained.) Don't do it.

Do Not Ask If She Wants to Or Needs to Go to The Bathroom.

Honestly, this is one of my biggest tricks with potty training. It seems so simple, but you will be amazed how hard it is to keep from asking your child if she wants to, or has to, go to the bathroom.

Asking your child, "Do you want to go potty?" allows the option to say "no." But really, there is no choice anymore. You've put her in underwear, so she needs to pee on the potty—no choice about it. And really, who wants to go to the bathroom? Even adults are annoyed by the task, yet we have to do it. If your child is in the middle of playing with a toy or doing something fun, she is never going to want to stop and go to the bathroom if you give her a choice. Never.

If you ask your child, "Do you need to go potty?" she really can't answer that honestly, so she will automatically tell you "no." Her little kidneys make about 10 drops of urine per minute, so really she could trickle out some pee whenever she sits down to try—kids just don't know that yet.

Instead of asking, replace the questions with the statement, "Tell me when you need to go potty." When you say this, it doesn't really require a response from your child, but she still hears the information and can now think about it and cue you when she needs to go.

I swear this works.

Do Not Expect Your Child to Tell You She Has to Go Before She Starts Peeing.

Okay, so now you know to say, "Tell me when you have to go potty." Realize, however, she isn't going to come right out and tell you ahead of time—for a while. As I said before, you are teaching a new habit and procedure. Your child is learning about her body. Once she grasps the concept and feels confident, she will be able to tell you when she needs to go. Some kids do this, two days after they start training, and others do this a week or two after starting.

Do Not Show Frustration or Anger.

Do not put your child into timeout or reprimand her for having an accident. It's really important to keep potty training as light and fun as possible. If you get angry with your child on a regular basis while in the bathroom, she will start to think you're always going to be angry in there. Fake it till you make it! Think about something happy, like the drink(s) you're going to have with (or instead of) dinner.

Do Not Give Your Child Her Reward Unless She Is Successful on The Potty.

I like to keep a child's reward in a glass jar on the middle of the counter where it can be seen. It's good for her to be reminded visually that she, too, benefits from this whole fiasco. There will be times when your child will see her treat and demand it. That's the time you firmly ask, "How can you get one of these?" If she doesn't answer, remind her that peeing on the potty will get her one and pooping on the potty will get her two. Stick to your guns, because if you give her a treat whenever, then she won't have any motivation to go use the toilet. You've already given her the treat, so what's the point?

Do Not Let Your Child Tell You "No."

There will be many times when you will have to give your child bathroom reminders or encourage her to go. You may, at some point, get a little pushback—usually in the form of a fit or a flat-out "no." If she does say "no," firmly respond, "Please do not tell me 'no.' Peeing in your underwear isn't a choice." Or, "Please do not tell me 'no.' You have to tell me when you need to go potty."

If your child throws a fit, try to push through it because, usually, it's just a stage to try to gain some control over the situation. If she has an accident, carry her to the bathroom (kicking and screaming and all), take off the wet underpants, and sit her on the potty. Try to keep her on the potty by distracting her with a song or telling her what a good job she is doing sitting on the potty.

If that doesn't work and the tantrum continues, take her off the toilet, thank her for sitting on the potty, and tell her, "We will try again in the future." Once she is cleaned up and completely calm from her fit, tell her that behavior is not okay and that time she has to tell you when she needs to go potty. It's appropriate for your child to apologize for throwing a tantrum. Give her a big hug, tell her how proud you are of her for being such a big kid today, and acknowledge how hard it can be. It's nice to be validated sometimes.

If your child throws a fit over something nontoilet related, just let her. Do not try to rationalize or bribe the child. Sit calmly beside her while she's throwing her fit, and once she starts to calm down, try to divert her attention to something new, such as an activity you can do together. Even if she doesn't want to play, if you start playing and acting like it's so much fun, chances are she will come over and join you. Tantrum over.

Don't Do This

- Do not ask if she has to or wants to go to the bathroom.

- Do not expect your child to tell you before she has to pee (at the beginning).

- Do not give back your child's diapers.

- Do not give her a reward unless she is successful on the toilet.

- Do not leave your child alone in a room.

- Do not let her tell you "no."

- Do not let your child watch TV or play on electronic devices.

- Do not show anger or frustration with your child.

- Do not use your phone for more than 15 to 30 seconds at a time

Chapter 8 - What are Things to Consider in Potty Training Girls

Frequency

Take your toddler to the toilet first thing after waking, before meals, before going out to play and coming in from playing. This will be about every 2 hours. I have seen many parents take their toddler every 5 minutes in the hope of catching something. This not only is very time consuming but becomes boring for the toddler.

There are three reasons for waiting in between visits:

1. The bladder does not have any time to fill and so your toddler does not learn to feel the sensation of fullness or learn to hold and let go. If she does, it is such a small trickle that it is hardly going to have any impact and may go unnoticed.

2. The novelty of potty training will wear off very quickly for both of you if you are at the bathroom door all day and don't leave time for anything else.

3. Going too frequently places an enormous amount of attention on the activity. Sometimes this makes your toddler feel that it is the most important thing for the whole family. This is fine if all is going well but if there are accidents, the toddler may feel as though she is not performing well and letting the side down.

Diaper on /diaper off?

Take the diaper off and use training underpants.

Little cotton pants which go up and down easily are ideal. Using the pull on and off diaper does not give your toddler any feeling of being wet or a little uncomfortable. (They can be used for outings).

Use loose clothing which can be pulled up and down easily. Let your toddler run around in just these training underpants or bare for a while. (Another reason to start in the warmer months).

Avoid a lot of attention to diaper changing time. Make it dull and boring now.

Avoid negative comments like "oh this is smelly" or "that's nasty" when changing dirty diapers or pants.

Rewards

Dull down rewards. A simple smile and hug is enough when your toddler has a try, regardless of the end result. Using food rewards should be avoided in all areas including potty training. Using stickers or big "prizes "in the early days can cause unnecessary disappointment.

What if I start the training and my little girl is not interested?

If you try all of these ideas for one week and your little one still has had not scored one basket, give it up for a few months and then try again. This is also a reason that we don't announce the initial training to the world. You don't want everyone asking how it is all going, if it is not.

Vocabulary

In reality it does not make a difference as to which words you use to describe the equipment used and substances produced by this equipment. Some parents wish to use the "correct" words from the beginning. This does avoid confusion. Many parents do not feel comfortable saying penis or vagina or even urine or bowel motion. Choose words which are commonly used so that when your toddler discusses things with others, they know she is talking about. Words like wee, pee or poop are common. You need to feel comfortable with your choices.

Diet

Always encourage your child to drink a lot of water. Being well hydrated is healthy and it increases your little girl's awareness of her bladder filling. Also, it is important to avoid constipation. The poop must be soft, and this encourages her to poop every day. Serve a good variety of fresh fruits and vegetables every day to boost healthy digestion.

Constipation

Constipation is when poop is hard or firm. Poop should be soft and formed. Constipation can lead to a build-up of gas and may cause cramping. Also, when passing a hard poop, your little girl might feel pain. This also means she may be reluctant to try to poop if she remembers the last time being painful. This can cause "holding on" which is very uncomfortable. Constipation also gives fewer opportunities to practice the exercise. So, this can make potty training for girls, take a little longer.

Wiping

You will need to wipe for your child initially. Let her flush the contents if she chooses and then encourage her to copy you in washing her hands afterwards. When wiping urine away, wipe from front to back. This avoids bringing any dirt forward which can get into the urinary tract, causing infections.

What about girls who choose to stand instead of sit?

Some girls become fascinated with the idea of standing to pee. They may have seen a sibling or boys at day care doing this. Explain that boys' and girls' parts are different. Girls pee down and boys pee out. Remind her about all those times she visited Mom while she was in the bathroom, that Mom is a girl and she sit too.

If she insists on standing, let her have a go. Remove all mats from the bathroom floor, shoes and all clothing in the line of fire. Most girls will find the "river "very uncomfortable and will go back to sitting.

Some children are afraid of the toilet. They are either afraid of the flush or of falling in or of being left alone. Most toddlers are egocentric and don't understand why you might not always want to share their joy. Do stay. Offer to read for them and give gentle encouragement. Never force her to sit as this will become a negative association and may delay training.

How long should she sit?

Keep it to about 4-5 minutes. If there is no result after this time, try again soon. Girls can become bored easily and less cooperative if she is kept away from play for extended periods.

Training for number two's

Although your little girl may feel the sensation of doing a poo before she realizes the sensation of doing a wee, the poo training generally comes second. Encourage this activity by beginning with positive statements such as "soon you will be able to try doing your poop in the potty.

If a child sits regularly and is relaxed, eventually something will drop into the pot. Once again, when this this happens, do help your little girl to phone your partner or Granny to show your excitement but do avoid posting it on Facebook.

If this is taking longer than you thought it might, don't punish or show your impatience. Have a break and try again in a few weeks.

What if my girl asks to do her poop in a diaper instead of the potty?

Some girls even though having mastered the art of peeing in the potty, may still ask for a diaper for the poop. Some will hold on for the night nappy to go on to make their deposit. Some parents find this very frustrating. My experience with this is to relax. Let your little girl know that at any time she feels a poo coming she can ask for a diaper. It is important that parents don't pressure children to only poop in the potty if they are still nervous about the process. This can lead to holding on and constipation. This will cause wind and cramping pain and yes you guessed it, a very unhappy toddler.

When your girl asks for a diaper, oblige but ask her to do it in the bathroom. This ways she becomes used to the appropriate place. Flush the contents down the toilet and go through hand washing too. If your girl has a fear of sitting on the toilet or potty, practice sitting there with the diaper on then practice doing the poop in the diaper while she sits on the toilet until she feels confident.

Some girls may continue this for some time. Be patient, don't pressure as your relaxed attitude will transfer to her, helping her.

Accidents

Learning any new skill takes practice. Sometimes your toddler may not make it to the potty or become so distracted by something that she forgets. Observe the body behavior of your little girl. Going quiet, squirming or wriggling can be signs of needing to go.

Day sleeps-Diaper or no diaper?

Most girls of this age are able to hold urine for about 1-2 hours which is the general length of a day nap. Try without the diaper but if there are accidents, use a diaper initially. Take it off as soon as she wakes and take her to the potty for a try.

Bed Wetting/ Nocturnal Enuresis

Bed wetting is more common than most people think but it can still cause anxiety for you and your little girl. When it seems every other girl at day care or parent's group is dry at night, it can be frustrating when your little girl has not quite made it there yet. The average age is about 3 years but 10% of 5-year-old children still bed wet every night.

It is important to realize that parents do not discuss this openly, but this means that in a class of 30 kindergarten children, 3 are still wetting regularly at night.

There is some genetic component to this. Often siblings or parents may have experienced the same. Night bed wetting is more common in boys and daytime wetting is more common in girls.

When do I start night training my girl?

The most appropriate time to begin is after a few nights of dry diapers. It is futile to start before the evidence is clear.

Aim for summertime as it is much easier for washing and middle of the night sheet changes. It is more comfortable for your girl and fewer layers of pajamas need to be worn. It is easier for parents to get out of bed to render assistance at 3am in the summer than in the winter.

Use a mattress protector. Some people believe in restricting fluids before bed. I believe in keeping your girl well hydrated during the day, but it is not necessary to fill the reservoir right before bed.

Do I sit her on the pot just before I go to bed?

Yes you can, and this works if she is awake enough to know what is happening and can be cooperative.

Wet bed/dry bed

Give praise for the dry bed and a gentle "oh well never mind" to the wet bed. Avoid big rewards and gifts. If your child has been promised a prize for a dry bed and tries really hard but still wets,

it can be devastating. She may understand the concept, know what to do and may really want to please you but she may sleep so soundly that she misses the signal. She may feel as though she   has   failed.
 Keep it simple. Don't set a date for the achievement. Although her mind may be ready and her spirit willing, her body may not yet be ready just yet.

Regression

My girl has been dry, for 3 months and now she wets most days.

This can occur due to physical illness, an infection or can be an emotional reason. The most common time for regression is when a new sibling is born. It can be attention seeking, excitement or due to mixed messages from parents. Your toddler may find it difficult to understand why a new baby wears a diaper and she has to go to the potty. Also, when parents make a fuss of the new baby at diaper change time, your toddler will want the same. She will not understand when you give different focus to her. Ignore accidents, praise her efforts at trying. Keep the new baby's change time less interesting. If your little girl goes completely in reverse, reinstate the diaper and try training her again in a few weeks.

Chapter 9 - How to Solve Potty Training Problems and Chart Progress

As a busy parent, you're trying to balance multiple responsibilities while potty training. When you first start, and even throughout the process, you won't be able to catch them all—accidents are bound to happen. Dealing with accidents is without question the most frustrating part of potty training. But know that they're a completely normal part of the learning process! Every child makes mistakes when learning a new skill. It's very important to be patient and not allow any personal frustration to show. Many people tend to keep track of the number of accidents during potty training as a way to gauge progress, but really you should only be keeping track of the successes.

In the very beginning, accidents are simply because your child doesn't yet possess the muscle control or awareness to make it to the potty in time. Once your child starts to understand the concept, accidents can still occur, and most of the time they're a result of distraction. If your child is engrossed in an activity, like playing outside, two things tend to occur. Number one, they're less aware of the sensation of needing to go potty until it starts happening, and number two, they'll hold it in, so they don't have to stop the activity, potentially until it's too late. Accidents are also more likely to occur when your child is sick, very tired, or overly excited.

Whenever your child says they need to use the potty, do your best to take them right away. When you first scrap the diapers, the time between your child realizing they need to go and the pee or poop actually coming out is only about 10 to 15 seconds, so you want to make sure you avoid the accident if possible. That way you can reward your child for three behaviors: recognizing their need to go, letting you know in time, and using the potty successfully!

No matter the reason for the accident, there should never be any shaming, scolding, or punishing. At the same time, you don't necessarily want to be too comforting either, because that could actually make your child falsely believe that accidents are acceptable. A minimal, matter-of-fact reaction works best. If you aren't able to catch any pee or poop in the potty once the accident starts, quickly acknowledge the situation by saying, "Oops, you peed on the floor. Remember, pee goes only in the potty now. Let's try harder to get there another time. Just tell me and I can help you." (You can use any combination of these statements).

When there is an accident, even if you think there's nothing left to come out, it's important to sit your child on the potty afterward as they may not have finished peeing or pooping. If they get anything in the potty at that point, still treat it as a success. Put most of your focus and attention on your child's positive potty behaviors and not as much on the negatives.

To avoid accidents when you're out and about, always encourage your child to use the potty before you leave and then again when you get to where you're going. Many children will say, "No, I don't have to go," but then will need to go at the least opportune time, such as when you're stuck in traffic on your way to drop them off at daycare. If you notice this to be true with your child, it's helpful to incorporate potty use into your daily out-the-door routine. Add using the potty to a short list of other tasks you direct your child to do. For example, you could say, "Please use the potty, put your shoes on, and say goodbye to Mommy." Always make sure to praise and/or reward their compliance.

If you find the accidents are persistent and you aren't seeing any improvement, it can help to exaggerate the cleanup process as much as possible. Make your child stop playing until everything is cleaned up and do a thorough wipe-down or bathe them before changing their clothes. This shows your child that using the potty is faster than going in their pants or on the floor. You can also have them participate in the cleanup if you think that would be a deterrent based on your child's personality. If you decide to try this tactic, remember it should not be used as a form of punishment, but rather as an automatic and consistent result to the behavior.

Occasionally some children will have small dribbles in their underwear before making it to the potty, not even enough to penetrate through to make their pants wet. This is normal and shouldn't be considered an accident. It's your child's way of testing the limits to see how long they can go before stopping and getting to the potty. Remind them to stop and go as soon as they feel the need. As their muscle control improves, this behavior will diminish.

Troubleshooting Techniques

My child is very attached to their diapers, and I'm worried they'll be upset about throwing them away.

If diapers are important to your little one, then just throwing them away in the garbage may not be the best option for you. To your child, those familiar white things that have been securely wrapped around them holding their pee and poop aren't just trash, so treat the diapers with a little more respect. Have your child help you box them up and wrap them like a gift, and then you can leave it on the front porch for the "mail carrier" to take to another family that needs them more.

My child refuses to sit on the potty!

This can be very frustrating, but it's important to remember that this whole potty-training experience is very new (and maybe even a little scary) for your child. If your child refuses to sit on the potty, that obviously makes it very difficult to potty train! You can warm your child up to sitting on their potty by showing their favorite doll or toy or a sibling sitting on it, or allowing them to pour water into the potty so they can see that when something goes in, nothing scary happens. Above all, take baby steps and do your best to use patience and reassurance to comfort your child's uneasiness.

My child sits on the potty, but nothing comes out!

First, put yourself in their shoes. Imagine if someone told you no more peeing and pooping on the toilet and to do it in a diaper instead. It would be hard for you to make that transition, right? So, if your child sits on the potty but doesn't release, your time may be better invested in just waiting for them to start going and then sitting them on the potty to finish. Once they see that they can do it a couple of times (even if it takes a little help from you), they'll feel more comfortable doing it on their own. Also, having your child blow bubbles or take deep breaths, turning on the tap (for the sound of running water), or placing your child's feet in a bowl of warm water are all effective tricks to encourage release!

Charting Progress

As I've already mentioned, it's important to pay attention to and learn your child's cues, behaviors, and potty language. You probably have a pretty good handle on all that at this point. But it's also going to be very valuable to jot these and other things down as you're working with your child so that when you go back to your regular routine, the transition is as seamless as possible when your child is in someone else's care. Things that you want to make note of include how much liquid your child drinks before needing to use the potty, how often your child tends to go potty (both pee and poop), and how long they're able to hold their bladder. You'll also want to note changes to their behavior when they need to use the potty and particulars about their potty preferences.

How Much Liquid Your Child Drinks Before Needing to Go to the Bathroom

You can gauge this by noting when you give your child something to drink, the approximate volume (don't get out a measuring cup or anything!), how long it takes them to finish the drink, and any times they use the bathroom in between. This important information will allow your child's caregivers to prompt them to use the potty at appropriate times, especially if your child isn't to the point of self-initiation just yet.

How Many Times per Hour Your Child Needs to Pee?

The easiest thing to do is to jot down each time your child pees over the first few days of potty training. Based on that, you should be able to see somewhat of a trend. You can pass this information on to your child's caregivers, so they'll know how often they should be prompting potty use, even if it differs some between mornings and afternoons. If things seem a bit all over the place (which it very well might at first), a general rule of thumb is every 30 minutes. But as your child gets further into the potty-training process, the time in between pees will gradually increase.

How Often Your Child Poops

There are two important things to note when it comes to poop timing: frequency (or number of poops per day) and time of day (i.e., first thing in the morning, mid-morning, lunchtime, evening, etc.). Most children are at least somewhat predictable when it comes to their poop timing and habits. However, keep in mind that during potty training, poop frequency naturally decreases. No one is really sure why, but it does certainly make things more convenient. Your twice-a-day pooper may go down to once a day or even every other day. And that is totally normal. Pass along your child's poop signals, schedule, and habits, so the caregiver can be on higher alert during those times.

How Long Your Child Can Hold Their Bladder

By "hold their bladder," I mean how long they can go from the time they indicate needing to use the potty until the pee actually comes. In the beginning, it's almost instantaneous, so your caregiver will need to take them to the potty as soon as they see your child's potty dance or as soon as your child says they need to go. But as the training process progresses, your child's control will increase, and you'll start to be able to ask them if they can wait to go until you have access to the potty for them.

How Your Child's Behavior Changes When They Need to Use the Potty?

By now you should have a pretty good grasp of how your child's behavior can indicate their need to go potty. Most children get antsy, lose the ability to listen or focus, or act out when they really need to use the bathroom. Write down things your caregiver can look for instead of just waiting for your child to communicate their need verbally.

Your Child's Potty Preferences

Include in your instructions to your child's caregiver things your child tends to do or enjoys doing while on the potty, so the caregiver can carry over the same activities consistently in the new environment. Examples include singing a certain song while sitting on the potty, using a small potty as opposed to the regular toilet, reading a particular reading material while they sit, and receiving certain rewards and reactions to their success. By maintaining these same practices even when your child is not in your care, they're sure to feel more comfortable using the potty in a different place.

Chapter 10 - How to Choose the Right Potty

A number of individuals believe that it would be confusing to the child to have a separate facility to go in. At times, the process of potty training involves the introduction and mastering of a potty chair, then moving up to an adapter seat which fits over the toilet until the young little girl is big enough for actually using the toilet on her own.

However, this is certainly not written in stone and a number of individuals tackle potty training in different ways. An available potty chair is a great tool to teach your child about various toilet habits. It is something that belongs to your little girl alone and this gives them a sense of ownership that means a lot.

There are quite a few different options available when looking for a potty chair. Getting a hold of the right one could make all the difference in being successful during the potty-training process.

According to proponents of the potty chair, the child develops a sense of independence given that parents do not have to lift the child to put your little girl onto the seat. In addition, it allows the child's feet to be planted squarely on the ground to bear down while pooping and she and she can support the arms of the chair as well.

As was said before, a potty chair obviously belongs to the child, so your little girl will be proud of possessing it. Selecting the most suitable potty chair should start as soon as the child gives an indication that is ready for potty training.

The child should be involved in picking out her very own potty chair. You could narrow down the choice to two or three types and allow your child to pick from among those. This could cause the child to be even more anxious to try the potty chair.

In the event that the potty is in the bathroom, both your child and you can use the toilet simultaneously. This might be a frightening thought for some parents because of privacy issues; however, this could be the difference in making potty training a success.

One of the disadvantages of the potty chair is that girls may also make a mess when they are in the beginning stages of the potty training with or without your supervision. Another thing to think about is the fact that the potty will have to be cleaned out by you or your child. Cleaning it out in the beginning could be a fun experience; however, over time the appeal will be lost for the child and maybe for you as well.

If you plan on allowing your child to use a potty chair, then you should purchase one prior to the beginning of training, so that it will become a familiar fixture for the child. In addition, personalizing the potty chair will make it more interesting and unique. Your child can do this by adding decals or stickers. Another option is using eye-catching letters to spell out the name of the child.

Allow your child to sit on the potty chair and let your little girl know that, for now, it is okay to be on the potty with clothes on until your little girl gets used to it. However, when it is potty training time, the chair will be used in the same way Mommy or Daddy uses the toilet.

In the event that you choose to use a potty chair, it would probably be great if you could get a version that looks like a miniature toilet. Prior to buying the potty chair, ensure that you are aware of how the potty is removed. Do not buy it if it is hard to remove the pot or if it must be tipped while being removed.

In the event that you would like a urine deflector, you should look for one that is removable and made from flexible plastic. Potty chairs that have deflectors are seemingly easier to come across than the ones without them; however, in the event that your child gets hurt by one while attempting to sit on the potty, your little girl may refuse to ever get back on the seat.

You should consider buying a floor model, which is stable and will not slide around. Additionally, you should think about purchasing more than one potty chair, particularly if there is more than one bathroom or you live in a two-story house. The additional potty chair could always be used when travelling in the car or left at the home of the grandparents.

It is important to note that if the potty chair is equipped with a tray, lifting the tray will be yet another step that the child will need to master.

For toddlers who are larger than average, you should think about purchasing an adult-sized camping portable potty.

There are a number of remarkably special potty chairs, which can make the experience of going to the bathroom an interesting and fun experience for the child. I have a friend who purchased a music box potty for her daughter, which made instrumental sounds whenever she pooped or peed in it.

There are also potty chairs, which will play music whenever the child uses it. There are potties that have shapes at the bottom, which change color whenever the child pees. There is a product that is available on the market, which is complete with the flushing handle and it mimics the noises of the toilet whenever it is flushed.

When you are thinking about the kind of potty chair to get for your child, it is important to note that the bells and whistles that are included on the chair could get old quickly. Particularly, this becomes evident when the child finds it fun to pour water into it, so that your little girl can hear the sounds that it makes.

You should expect to pay between $12 and $100 for a potty chair. The least expensive ones you will find are typically plain and they do not have any additional features; however, they will get the job done. High priced potty chairs are generally made out of wood and there are models that resemble toilets from the Victorian Age.

Regardless of the kind of potty chair that you choose, ensure that child likes it. I believe that among the reasons that Matt hated sitting on the potty chair was because she was not interested in it. The chair was generic and had a lid that could be lifted and a removable bowl. Now I wonder if we would have had an easier experience if we had bought a Sponge Bob or Nemo chair.

We advocate taking the child along when picking out the potty chair and as soon as it is home, make a casual introduction. It is okay if the child would like to play with it for a while. Show your little girl how it works and have conversations regarding how your little girl is supposed to utilize it.

Ensure that a big deal is made about the fact that your little girl has something of their own which can be and should be used by young little girl. You should try to put the potty chair in a room in which your little girl plays often and make sure that you supervise.

Encourage the use of the potty by placing a chart on the fridge. Tell your child that every time that your little girl uses the potty, you will give out a sticker. That will serve as an incentive for using the potty chair. Children are fond of getting rewards.

There is another option to use while undertaking the potty-training process:

Toilet Adapter Seats

This is an alternate form of potty-training device and it is essentially a separate seat, which is placed over the regular toilet seat and makes it easier for the child to sit on the toilet. These kinds of seats could allow the child to have a deeper sense of security while using the toilet; however, it should be kept in mind that your little girl still has short legs. Getting on the toilet could be a challenge for your toddler; therefore, you should buy a stool, which your little girl can use to get on the toilet. In addition, stools could assist the kid in pushing with her very own legs while having bowel movements.

There are adapter seats that are available with built-in stepstools that are in the style of folding ladders. In the event that this works for the child, you should definitely take advantage of the technology.

The adapters are portable and lightweight and with these devices there is the extra advantage of flushing directly, which eliminates the need for additional cleaning up. However, adapter seats could become a nuisance for other members of the family if only one bathroom is in the house.

A number of adapter seats are available with straps for additional safety, in the event that the child will be left on the seat alone for any period of time. In the initial training stages, the child must never be left alone. If your little girl is strapped in place and left alone, it is very likely that the child will feel as if your little girl is being punished; ensure that you stay with your child.

In the event that the desired result is not achieved within five minutes, you are not going to. As the responsibility of using the adapter seat is taken on by the child, your little girl will be on and off without assistance in no time and there will no longer be any need for the straps.

You could consider purchasing a folding or an inflatable adapter seat to use when shopping or traveling, in spite of the method that is used at home.

Utilizing a type of potty chair that is inserted will make cleaning up much easier, given that all that will be required is flushing the toilet and maybe wiping off the seat.

A number of parents like that the inserts are portable. However, a major shortcoming is that a number of kids are initially afraid of the toilet insert. For the most part, these inserts are inexpensive; therefore, they may be worth trying.

Chapter 11 - How to Make Potty Training Fun and Educational

How To Make Potty Training Fun?

There are several things many parents often do while potty training in order to make the process more fun and enjoyable for their children. These will help the child grasp the process faster as they are more engaged. These include;

Potty training incentive charts. This is one of the most commonly used strategies used by parents in order to get their children more excited. You could stick up a chart in the bathroom or the child's room. On the charts should be clearly written potty training incentive chart.

You will need to buy fun stickers from your local store. Every visit your child makes to the potty should earn them a number of stickers which you will paste together on the potty incentive chart.

When the stickers reach a certain number like 5, the child should be rewarded for their efforts. This reward could be in the form of a toy or a cookie, or anything the kid loves.

Potty targets. Kid stores have flushable plastic shoot targets molded in the shape of fun things such as animals. These targets are small and will not affect the plumbing if you are worried.

This is a great way especially among girls to get them to aim properly while peeing into the potty or the toilet. When the child feels an urge to pee, these targets are put in the potty or toilet and the child has fun aiming for them while peeing.

If you cannot get the targets from the store, consider using cereal pieces, especially the round ones. This will make peeing more fun.

Plastic stools. These are a great way of helping your child pee into the big potty which is the toilet. This will also be easier for you as there will be little splashing like with most potties.

Plastic stools are also very light, and your child could move them around, from the toilet to the sink where they can wash their hands with ease. This is a small step but a giant leap for the child towards doing things on their own as they all love.

Another trick embraced by most parents is adding food color to the waters in the potty or toilet just before the child goes to pee.

The food color often changes color to green when the child empties their bladder into the potty.

This color change often amazes the children and they are therefore more interested in trying it over and over. This is a smart way to ensure your child pees into the potty.

Travel potties. Today there are several potties in the market. There are some that are designed to make it easier to carry around and travel around with. This ensures you will not have any trouble even if you go out with your child.

Even if you at the church or park or at work, there is no need of worrying that your child will make a mess. You will just have to carry along the travel potty and use it when the child feels an urge to urinate or empty their bowels.

Music. There are several potty songs that that could be used to motivate the child along in potty training. You could come up with a song to help relax the child when they are sitting on the potty so that they can empty their bowels with much more ease.

Also come up with a song to be sung after the child is done saying that she managed the great task. This song offers praises, a thing most children will respond most positively to. There are also potties in the market which start singing whenever a child sits on them. This makes the process more fun and the child naturally enjoys the process of potty training.

Treats and toys. Most children will respond well when there is a reward at the end of the potty trip. This makes them eager to use the potty every time they feel pressed. You could go to the toy store and pick several toys and treats, place them in a bag which is opaque.

Every time your child uses the toilet, you can let them pick a reward from the bag. For most girls, the best way is to involve their toy dolls. You could buy a spare potty to be used by the girl, explaining that the dolls did not need diapers as they used their potty properly. This is bound to work as your child will be motivated to do the same.

For other parents, they preferred drawing a race track every time their child used the potty, they put a fun sticker along the racetrack. When the stickers reached the end of the racetrack, the child was given a reward by picking any favorite toy they wanted.

Putting the child in charge. This often helps with children who love doing things as the like. You could begin by setting half hour reminders and asking the child if they felt pressed and needed to use the potty. They will tell you what they need. If no, wait a while longer.

Some children also prefer being left to take of their clothes and use the potty. With time as they get older, some get sensitive. Some will ask to let the door open. Keep the door open as it helps them feel at ease. Others prefer locking the door and flushing the toilet.

Let them do this as it gives them a sense of achievement. Let your child take the lead once they get the hang of it.

Stop using diapers. As the child grows, resist the temptation of having them in nappies all the time. If you are worried about your furniture and carpets, you could have them covered in painters' plastics to help in cleaning in case of any accidents.

Also avoid using training nappies all the time as children do not feel uncomfortable in them, hence potty training might take a longer.

It would even be more advisable to use cloth nappies which when soiled, makes them quite uncomfortable and the child quickly realizes the need to use the potty.

For girls, it will be easier to have them in dresses. These make the child's work lighter when they need to use the potty. Most nappies may be difficult to get out of.

Pants. Most children see having pants a big deal and look forward to having them on. You should take your child shopping to pick a set of pants they admire. To make it fun, pick pants with favorite story characters with names they lack.

This will help your child notice when they wet themselves and will always try to use the potty. Pants are also an easier alternative to get out of when using the potty.

The pants with characters could be named according to the character. Constantly remind the child not to wet their favorite story character.

Teaching Your Child Proper Hygiene

This is a very important step especially if a child is going to use the toilet or potty without any supervision. The health of a child is very important and most of the time it hinges on hygiene.

It is very easy for a child to get the hands dirty when using the potty or toilet. It is important that the child is taught how to wipe themselves using toilet tissue from front to back. Every time your child uses the potty, you could wipe them then let them wipe themselves.

This will help them practice and perfect on it. They should know how to hold the toilet paper and how much they need every time. This will help keep those hands they often stick in their mouths clean. The child will also need to learn how to wash their hands when they are done.

To help your child wash their hands, there are a couple of strategies you could use to help them along. To start off, you could show your child how to wash the hands after using the potty or toilet. For this, you will need those plastic stools that will help them reach the sink.

You can wash your hands alongside them. Show them how to use the hand wash to scrub the hands and fingers thoroughly for a sufficient time.

Once you have shown them a couple of times how it is done, you could include it in the potty challenge. They will only get a reward for using the potty and washing their hands thoroughly after that.

Hygiene is important and encourages your child to wash very other time, not only when they use the potty. This will help the habit of thoroughly wash the hands be ingrained in then. They will then embrace it every time even without thought when they use the toilet.

To make hand washing more fun, you could introduce a sparkly and colorful kid-friendly hand washing detergents to get your child excited about washing their hands. The duration of hand washing is important. Children of lack a sense of time and to help them know how long to wash their hands, a song could be helpful.

An example is the alphabet song, to be sung during hand washing. This will help them be excited whenever they are washing their hands. There other songs that emphasize on hygiene and keeping your hands clean. The bathrooms are full of bacteria and you need to teach your child how to avoid infections.

The Importance of Offering Praise

The all-important step in potty training is maintaining a positive attitude. This will go a long way in making your work easier and the child more inclined to learn faster. Never be cross with your child for soiling their pants and themselves while potty training.

You might think your child is fully potty trained and you might be surprised when they mess up. When you do so, you get them scared and the potty training will definitely take much longer than expected. So, despite challenges and set-backs you might face, it is very important that you keep a positive attitude and commend your child for trying to make it.

When your child uses the potty successfully, be sure to offers praises and a little reward. This is a milestone in the child's life and should be celebrated. Make sure the child knows you acknowledge what they have done and what it means to you. Praises such as, "you are now a big girl" and, "yaay! You did it" go a long way in assuring the child you are impressed even more than the toys and treats.

Potty Training Away from Home

Most children are leery of using any toilets or potties away from home. This is perfectly normal as every bathroom looks different. The toilets in most places also look big and to a toddler quite scary.

Some toilets also have automatic flashing units which might quite be scary to a toddler. All these contribute to making the using the toilets away from home quite a hard task for a child. Most children therefore end up soiling and wetting themselves when away from home, maybe when at school.

The child has to learn eventually how to use the toilets away from home. This will come in handy especially when they start schooling. To help the child get used to toilets away from home, get them started with one that is familiar, a place away from home.

It should be a place they feel comfortable and relaxed even though it is away from home. This could be at their grandparents' home or a friend's home. To help them along, carry along the portable travel potty or toilet seat-reducer potty.

Chapter 12 - How Important is Communication in Potty Training and Other Tips?

Importance of Elimination Communication

Elimination Communication is the practice that involves making use of your child's cues to greatly help them get rid of their waste. For some, it appears like zero diaper use ever, while for others, it's a mixture of using diapers. It doesn't actually matter how long you've used EC or how regular.

Now, you're scanning this, which means no matter current EC literature, you understand in your heart, it's sure for completion. I'm likely to call this completion procedure a "bridge," for brevity; a bridge from there to here.

I actually contacted some EC specialists because increasingly more people wish to potty train before twenty weeks. I completely support this but discovered this might be a particular percentage of Elimination Communication and a specific percentage of Potty training.

However, below are several things that are part of EC that may make potty training a little difficult.

1. Diaper-free Time.

2. Getting the pee, not shifting to the potty.

3. Philosophy.

4. The idea that your child or daughter will simply potty train themselves.

5. The expectation that EC offers you a joint potty training.

6. Potty strike.

Diaper-free Time

We don't know about your position but also for many parents, Diaper-free Period gets misconstrued. For most, Diaper-free time probably condition your child or daughter to pee on to the floor.

I've heard many tales of children who just stay naked all day long with parents attempting catches but really just clearing up a whole lot of pee. I talked to numerous EC experts over time. I couldn't wrap my head for this particular practice.

There's just therefore much to learn that every moment can be an experiment and discovery. So, if they pour their milk away on the ground, it's for the pleasure of viewing, "Oh . . . this occurs when I do that. Great."

Nevertheless, it's our work as parents to tell them that

pouring milk on the floor isn't suitable. While we wouldn't yell or shame them, we'd consistently most likely frown and say something comparable to, "No, no . . . zero milk stays up for grabs."

So, now let's consider the cause and after-effect of peeing anywhere, anytime the desire hits. If you never let your kid know that it's unacceptable, you won't likc the aftermath effect. It's consequently learned behavior to simply pee where you have to pee. This may be okay in the first days, whatever age group you started elimination communication, but once your child regularly does this for just about any big chunk of period, it's kind of cemented in. In other terms, you've traded a diaper for your floor.

The only reason I talk about Diaper-free Time is since the initial thing I hear from an EC Mama is level of resistance to a naked day time.

The naked day time is quite crucial to one of the largest steps in building the bridge from EC to PT, which lead us to issue number 2.

Getting Pee, and not on a Potty

So far in EC, you almost certainly have an incredible bond with your child. You understand her signals and you hurry to take her potty, mostly where it's convenient. I really like the actual fact that EC offers you "permission" to potty anywhere. Nevertheless, once you officially begin potty schooling, you do need to get your child or daughter to the potty of choice (either the tiny potty or the place on the toilet). The big thing here's getting the child physically to the correct place. However, the norm is to be getting the kid to the potty. I'd say this task alone may be the biggest in the bridge from there to here.

Philosophy

I understand that "traditional potty schooling" is a dirty term in EC. I understand there are "shoe camps" for potty training and all types of coercive methods or advice. However, at times I discover myself having to remind parents that it's alright to possess boundaries and objectives. There's a whole lot of philosophy around

EC and attaching parenting that sometimes falls aside as your child or daughter nears the twos. I don't think the twos have to be terrible by any stretch, nevertheless, you may find that a few of this EC-associated philosophy doesn't endure. I don't wish to argue this aspect, and I'm not really saying anything about anyone's parenting design. I just find this as certainly a difficult place in parenting to keep up theory. Your child will begin limit screening, and her favorite word is going to be "No."

Most of the philosophy suggests that there may be nothing bad around the potty.

Very much as in the "milk on to the floor" cause-and-effect example, you do need to tell your child or daughter what your positive expectation is and what the adverse expectation is. This doesn't have to sound mean, but you do have to mean business. At some time, your child must find out that peeing simply anywhere is a "don't." A lot of parents emphasize the positive end of issues ("just pee in the potty"), but they omit the other section of the equation ("don't pee somewhere else"). Therefore, yes, you definitely want to emphasize the positive, but be sure you are getting clear in what you don't need as well.

Expecting Your Toddler to Potty Train on Her Own

Occasionally a child will opt to potty herself. Generally, this is simply not the case, however, which makes feeling if you think about any of it. And that's most likely why you are right here. Peeing and pooping are primal behaviors, do you agree? You don't need to teach a child how exactly to pee or poop. Placing it in a container of some kind is a socialized behavior. Socialized behavior should be taught, the simplest way to obtain it is to slap it all out of your hands. That's primal. The socialized way of setting it up is to ask or negotiate. That's what should be taught.

How do we train that?

When our kids utilize the primal instinct to slap something out of someone's hand, we gaze at them in the eye, we say in a fairly stern voice, "Zero hitting. You ask." We most likely frown or make a disapproving facial expression. We are far better whenever we use simple vocabulary. "No this, Yes that." There doesn't have to be a ton of discussion about this. I think most of us, as a whole are doing a significant amount of talking. I specifically think that is true in potty teaching. It's similar to your girl or daughter learning the ABCs. They aren't learning all of the power behind the letters that produce different sounds at differing times in an incredible number of combinations. In potty training, the brief, more direct words function best.

The Expectation That Elimination Communication Offers You Potty Training

I believe bridging EC with PT is the hardest part with respect to coping with the expectation that because you've been functioning at this for a reasonably long time, this will become easy for your girl or daughter. Trust me, I think this will be true as well. I don't desire you to end up being mad at me, but I've discovered that this isn't necessarily the case. It's a genuine freaking bummer.

And the actual fact that you're most likely not to get one is actually hard to wrap your mind around. What I've found is that once you're more than the hump, ECed children tend to move considerably faster and the training "sticks" far better. And you possess the bonus of not just a great relationship but also of understanding your child's signals.

Teaching the Vocabulary

Throughout your everyday events, coach your toddler, the phrases and meanings of toilet-related terminologies such as body parts, urination, bowel motions, and toilet duties. When enough time comes for real potty schooling, there is so very much to learn, so that it will be useful if the young child currently is more comfortable with the necessary information.

Lots of terms that are used during potty training aren't directly toilet-related but can make different concepts for your girl or daughter to comprehend. Descriptive words that you'll use during the procedure are those like wet, dry, clean, flush, and toilet paper (tissue paper).

Teach your child the idea of opposites and specific purposes which will give a foundation for toilet training. Wet/dried out, on/off, messy/clean, up/down, stop/proceed, now/later, these are concepts that'll be part of the potty-training routine.

It's common for parents to employ a mixture of phrases and terms during the potty process but doing this can confuse a fresh trainee. If for instance, you question her if she would "go potty," however, the next day you asked her "to go use the toilet," and later consult her if she must "pee," she might not follow your school of thought. It is best if you choose your vocabulary conditions and adhere to them during the training process.

Keep the Training Natural

Babies and also toddlers accept things that happen in their diaper as normal and natural. It is not until siblings, peers, and adults instruct them there's some factor disgusting about these procedures that they think in another case. Try to let your child or daughter maintain this innocent viewpoint about elimination. This can help toilet teaching, and potty training becomes a more definite knowledge without any embarrassment or shame.

Don't attach negative worth to wet or messy diapers. (Ensure you avoid words like miserable, icky, stinky or smelly) Do not make a significant creation about the smell or consistency and do your very best to caution your child or daughter's big brothers and sisters about this!

The Worthiness of Demonstrations

It can be beneficial to let your child see you or her siblings utilize the toilet. You won't need to have her view every detail; it's much enough to have her discover you take a seat on the toilet bowl while you explain what you are doing. Tell her that whenever she gets heavily pressed, she'll place her pee-pee and poo-poo in the toilet, too, rather than in her diaper.

If your child or daughter has older siblings, cousins, or friends, tell her that they used diapers when they were her age, however now they utilize the toilet. If they're available to accompany in the toilet, let your baby get a glimpse of her other older sibling or peer using the potty. Allow her to understand that when she gets just a little older, she'll produce that act, too.

Don't assume all parent is ready to have little eye viewing while they utilize the toilet, and it's not essential for you to do that. If you like your privacy, after that teach your child or daughter to respect a shut bathroom and toilet door. Remember that as your child or daughter masters her very own toileting, she is more likely to stick to in your footsteps and desire her personal privacy as well. Set up the toilet so that it's safe and sound and manageable on her behalf and keep hearing open when she actually is alone in the toilet.

Carefully Select Your Potty Words!

Certain words are normal in particular geographic areas, plus some are more trusted than others. If you pay attention to daycare, the recreation center, or the retail shopping center, you'll soon know very well what words are normally used in town.

Chapter 13 - What are Myths and Misconceptions about Potty Training

In 1964, diaper manufacturers were pondering the many ways that they could innovate diapers in general and also add convenience for the parents. The result? Disposable diapers. Most parents have found this innovative design useful. While many of us even wonder what we would have done without it, it is important to remember that disposable diapers have been around for less than 60 years. Yet mothers have been potty training their children long before disposable diapers came into existence, so most children were potty trained by the age of 12-18 months. The constant washing of pants and clothes might seem like a big project to many parents today, but a few decades ago, it was just another chore that parents would accomplish.

Before we start looking at what we should be doing or believing about potty training, it is best we understand what we shouldn't.

This allows us to approach potty training with better insights and knowledge.

At this point, it is important to understand that people who believe in these myths are no less smart than those who don't. Parents don't believe in myths because they want to; they do so because they want to make sure that they are doing everything they can to give the best life for their children. It is for this reason that when a child so much as coughs, a parent's heart starts beating like a heavy metal drum solo at a rock concert. Parents worry about every little thing and because of this worry, it is easy for them to believe certain things.

If you are guilty of believing any of these myths, then do not worry. You are not going to be labeled anything for wanting to do and be the best for your child. Besides, you did make an effort to be better informed. Shouldn't that tell you how awesome you are for wanting to know more for your child?

In order to under these myths better, I am going to present you a series of statements. I would like you to go through them and think about which statements you think are true, either because you heard rumors, read an article online, feel they sound like common sense, or for any other reason. This is a judgment-free zone. So, don't feel bad that you believe in one or many of the statements mentioned below.

When your child or daughter is ready, she will start showing interest in toilets.

Simply making your child sit on the potty will train your little girl.

It takes less time to potty train girls.

You should potty train your child by the age of (insert age).

It is better to train your child to pee first before training your little girl to poop.

Myth #1

When your child or daughter is ready, she will start showing interest in toilets.

Reality

What child isn't interested in toilets. To them, it is a bowl filled with water. And what's that?! The water disappears down a hole! So fascinating!

To children, the toilet is a mysterious phenomenon that has the wondrous ability to make water move around. On the subject of water, is that something to dip one's hands in? You might answer no. Well, children might have a different opinion since some of them might try to reach into the bowl to dip their hands into the water. To their beautiful and innocent minds, a toilet is a curious object filled with wonders to be unlocked. If they are showing interest in them, then perhaps it is because they are interested in the toilet itself and not an action related to it.

Myth #2

Simply making your child sit on the potty will train your little girl.

Reality

Quite a few parents believe that simply making the child sit on the potty will prompt your little girl to immediately figure out its mechanics. In some cases, the parents lead a busy life and are often feeling exhausted to think about potty training. In other cases, it is simply because parents are unaware that there are ways to potty train a child (thankfully, you are making efforts to study the process).

Even advertisements about potty trainers simply show the parent placing the child on the potty training and the following scene reveals the child smiling wide, having completed pooping. It does not work that way. It does look simply and the simplistic messaging of more advertisements often make parents feel bad about their efforts. They begin to doubt if they are doing it right.

Many of them don't question the fact that perhaps they are not training their children the right way. Surely if it is so easy in the advertisements, then it has to be easy in real life, right?

Even if the child or daughter does not resist sitting on the potty, it does not mean that she has figured out how it works.

Myth #3

It takes less time to potty train girls.

Reality

This myth has been in existence for a long time and no one seems to do anything to correct it. Perhaps it is because of the idea that girls mature faster than boys. That might be true during preteen years, but all children develop at their own pace, regardless of their sex. Parents need to realize that each child is going to learn potty training differently. I have personally seen cases where the boys had been potty trained at a certain age but the girls, being of the same age as the boys, were still figuring things out. But using that as an example to highlight intelligence and maturity is a flawed observation.

Let's try and approach this myth from another perspective. Here are the three common ways that developmental psychologists study children.

Cross-Sectional Studies

In this method, psychologists compare the abilities or behaviors of two or more groups of children. These groups can either have something in common or they might have entirely different characteristics.

Longitudinal Studies

Psychologists follow the lives of children across a period of time, even well into their adulthood. The psychologists do not interfere with the lives of the children and merely conduct interviews at certain intervals to discover more information about their lives.

Case Studies

Either one or a small number of children are seen regularly over a period of time. The time period could be anywhere from six months to a period longer than one year. The difference between this and the above form of study is that in the former method, the psychologists do not interfere too much. In this method, the psychologists make periodic visits in a careful manner so that they don't affect the normalcy of the people they are studying.

If you look at the above methods, then you might notice a common trait among them; they are all based on observational methods. None of them include psychological experiments.

Now, why would that be? You and I both might have the same thought for that question; what a ghastly thing to do to a child? How could one think of even subjecting children to psychological experiments?

And that is true. Children's minds are delicate. Unless the psychologist knows what your little girl is doing, they might inadvertently affect children's behavior.

But that also tells us something important; it is not easy to predict the mind of a child. A does not always equal B. Children are complex and one cannot make casual remarks about their behavior. Just because a child took the time to learn to walk does not mean they are less intelligent. Such distinctions only serve to cause unwanted worry and stress for parents.

In a similar way, do not think too much about the learning abilities of your child if you have a daughter. Whether they learn quickly or slowly depends on various factors, and none of them indicate the level of maturity of your child.

Myth #4

You should potty train your child by the age of (insert age).

Reality

As we had already seen, children become ready for potty training anywhere between 18 months to up to 3 years. If you have been coming under pressure because you have been listening to advice or looking at articles that either claim that there is a "right age" for potty training, then take a deep breath. There is nothing to worry about.

The truth about potty training is that it is like any other skill that your child picks up, including reading, speaking, and walking. With your support, your child will work things out at their pace.

Myth #5

It is better to train your child to pee first before training your little girl to poop.

Reality

It is easy to see why parents would think that getting a child to accomplish one task would automatically help your little girl to complete the other. After all, it does seem easier to help your child pee better before your little girl learns to poop. Human beings pee more times during the day than they poop. We drink more water during the day and some of the foods that we eat (including green vegetables) have water content in them. Excess water is usually flushed out by the body regularly. This also means that there are more chances to teach a child to pee properly than poop. However, the two are completely different in not just the way they feel, but also in the time taken to complete them. This is why, when you teach a child potty training, you are also telling them to be patient. While this is not always the case, sometimes children think that pooping takes the same time as peeing, especially if they were trained to pee first.

Other Misconceptions

Misconception: Children Must Remain Dry Throughout the Night

Many parents wrongly assume that they haven't potty trained their children properly because the children wet their beds during the night. This is not true. Children can be independent during the day when it comes to their toileting skills. However, they could continue to wet the bed at night. Let us assume that your child sleeps for about eight hours every day. That gives your little girl a sixteen-hour window to empty the bladder. However, that is something you and I, as adults, know and have trained our bodies to realize. Since you have just begun to potty train a child, it might take a while for your little girl's body to adjust to a certain time cycle. So, don't worry too much if your child is wetting the bed. It does not automatically indicate poor potty-training skills.

Misconception: Potty Training is Not Just Peeing

When you are teaching a child to use the toilet, you must allow the child every opportunity to not just pee but poop as well. Sometimes, as the child is peeing, she might feel like taking care of her bowel movements as well. Allowing her to sit in order to pee will give her the opportunity to poop as well, if she wants to do so.

Misconception: Children Must be Able to Dress Themselves After Using the Potty

We are so used to dressing ourselves up after using the facilities that we don't realize that it is actually an extra step we perform after using the toilet. Teaching the child to dress themselves should be done separately as the sole focus of potty training should be about pooping and peeing.

Misconception: Children Should Always Use the Portable Potty Before Using the Toilet

When it comes to potty training, the main focus is on giving the child every opportunity to become successful. Although the use of a portable potty might be beneficial to some, other parents might not have the ability to use portable potties. In such cases, there are numerous child-safe toilet attachments that parents can use to train their children.

Chapter 14 - What are Popular Potty-Training Methods and Techniques

Method 1: Going Bare-bottomed

The Basis: The basis of this method is formed from the premise that children do not like to wet themselves. By letting them go around fully naked or just bare from the waist down, they will be able to figure out how to use the potty by themselves.

The Application:

Set aside ample time for the training process of at least six hours.

Remove the child's clothes from the waist down and allow your little girl to play.

Let the child drink a lot of fluids and basically create a number of opportunities for "going potty." Do these while keeping the child within easy access of the potty receptacle. This can be done by doing the potty training in a closed room or in the backyard.

Stay with the child but make sure not to ask your little girl to have a seat on the potty.

Let the child figure things out all on her own.

The Disadvantages: Potty training accidents can be very messy.

Tips to Be Effective:

- Potty train in a room or area that is easy to clean.

- If you choose to stay in the backyard, choose a warm day.

- Avoid lecturing your child while cleaning up.

Method 2: The Child-Oriented Method

The Basis: Parent-led techniques are pushing children to potty train before they are ready. This leads to problems like constipation, refusal to use the toilet, and stool smearing. The right approach should be gradual.

The Application:

Do not start toilet training unless your child is ready and exhibits spontaneous signs of being so.

Before starting on a series of steps, make sure that the child shows an interest. If the child reacts in a negative way, stop and wait until your little girl is interested. It is the child who sets the pace for potty training.

The Steps are:

Step One: Allow the child to choose her very own personal potty

Step Two: Encourage the child to sit on the potty while fully clothed.

Step Three: Empty the child's soiled diaper into the potty and encourage the child to wash her own hands clean after.

Step Four: Successfully using the potty will happen spontaneously.

The Disadvantages: The potty-training timeframes vary but this method usually takes a very long time.

Tips to Be Effective:

Encourage potty use by allowing the child to go around naked from the waist down while keeping the potty chair in visible areas.

The goal is to let children think that potty training is their spontaneous idea.

Method 3: The Wait and See Method

This is similar to the child-oriented method in that the child is supposed to make the initiative when your little girl is ready to use the potty.

The Application:

When your child is about two years old, watch for signals that your little girl is ready for potty training.

Put a potty seat near or in the bathroom but do not insist that your child use it.

Be supportive and praise your child when your little girl uses the potty.

Method 4: The Planned Potty-Training Method

The Application:

A specific timetable is set purely for potty training. This can be form one day to one week.

The concept is like a boot camp that focuses on potty training.

The child is taught how to recognize sensations and urges related to using the potty or toilet. Your little girl is then steered towards the right direction and right actions to do.

The Disadvantages: Of your child easily gets distracted or frustrated, this method can be a little intense.

Method 5: The Transition from Training Pants Method

The Application:

Replace diaper use with the use of disposable potty-training pants.

Ask your child often if your little girl needs to use the bathroom.

Give the child praise every time your little girl uses the potty on time.

Another alternative is to use diapers with a "wet sensation" and instruct the child to tell you when the diaper gets cool.

The Advantages:

Accidents are effectively contained

The child becomes aware of her body's functions.

The Disadvantages: It is not cost effective and environment friendly.

Method 6: The Prize and Reward Method

The Application:

Start by using any other method of your choice.

Give rewards such as a sticker every time your child succeeds in using the potty.

The Advantages: Rewards are very motivating for children.

The Disadvantages: Children might ask to be compensated for everything they do right.

Method 7: The Underwear Technique

The Application: Allow your child to pick out any underwear or undergarment of your little child's choice. Let your child wear them and allow potty accidents happen freely.

The Advantages: Children will feel like grown-ups which in turn make them feel potty accidents acutely. Potty training is usually over quickly.

The Disadvantages: The potty-training process can be very messy.

Method 8: The Praise-Dependent Method

The Application: Praise your child every time your little girl uses the potty successfully. Relatives can also be asked to cooperate for more praises.

The Advantages: Praising builds confidence and self-esteem. The extra attention can be very motivating for children as well.

The Disadvantages: The child may feel discouraged when potty accidents happen.

Method 9: Infant Potty-Training Method

The Basis: Infant potty training can begin for babies that are just a few weeks old from birth. The indications or actions that signal when they are hungry and/or tired are the same as when they need to go to the bathroom.

The Application:

The baby's parents learn the indications and cues that their child needs to use the toilet. This is called as elimination communication.

When they recognize the indications or cues from their baby, the child is held over a potty or toilet to allow them to do their business.

The Advantages:

The process of potty training is done immediately. This makes training easier as the autonomous personality of toddlers is bypassed.

It promotes early bonding between child and parent.

Starting out early means finishing potty training early as well.

Cost effective and environment friendly with less use of diapers

Prevention of diaper-related problems like rashes

The Disadvantages:

Some experts argue that babies are too underdeveloped to actually be able to have appropriate bladder and bowel control required for potty training.

It can be messy

You have to stay with your baby every hour of every day.

Method 10: Practice Makes Perfect

This is a combination of several other methods as it also espouses the use of rewards and transitioning from diapers to regular underwear. It involves making the child practice as much as possible gradually and at your little girl's own pace.

The Advantages:

Less messy as it allows children to be in diapers until they transition to wearing regular underwear.

The Disadvantages:

The potty-training process can take a lot of time

Children might not learn to initiate going to the bathroom by themselves.

Trying to keep a child's attention for long periods of time is difficult.

Other Potty-Training Methods:

Potty training through pretend playing: A doll or toy is used to demonstrate the process of using a toilet

Giving positive reinforcements for good behavior such as food rewards or treats

Practice Drilling: Making children perform practice drills or runs for potty training accidents.

Potty Training for Girls

Once your child is ready to start potty training, try to focus on the right timing. Choose a time period where her routine is relatively well-established. Also, try to avoid those times when her natural resistance as a toddler is high. It is better to wait until she is open and more receptive to trying new ideas.

Potty Training Steps for Girls:

Allow your child to watch any female family member while she uses the toilet. Let her learn by imitation.

Let her get used to the idea of sitting on a potty or training seat. Make sure she is comfortable and try to make thing easier for her as much as possible: padded seats, a stool to help her, provide potty training studies, etc.

Teach your child how to wipe properly. Demonstrate and explain what she needs to do. Make sure that she learns how to wipe from front to back after each bowel movement. Patting the genital area dry after passing urine is also important.

Note 1: Try to be consistent and accurate. If you give a child-sounding name to her genitals while every other body part has a formal-sounding name, she may be confused. In the worst-case scenario, she may feel that something is wrong or embarrassing about her genitals.

Note 2: When your child sees someone from the opposite gender passing urine standing up, chances are she would want to try it as well. It is completely normal, and you should not say anything that would make her feel ashamed or inadequate. Gently explain to her why women and girls pass urine sitting down. She will eventually realize that she cannot properly use the toilet standing up.

Note 3: Girls are at risk for developing urinary tract infection during the potty stage due to incidents of holding in urine and to not wiping in the proper way.

Note 4: Putting girls in dresses or skirts can help them "go potty" faster and easier.

Technique in case of Toilet avoidance and toilet phobia

This problem is characterized by a potty-training child who refuses to sit on the toilet or potty. Initially, the refusal is done without any explanation. On occasion, the child may say that your little girl is afraid to take a seat on the toilet. The causes of the fear or phobia are:

- Painful bowel movements

- Having formerly experienced pain while having an enema or given a rectal suppository

- Being punished while being on the toilet

Your child might not be afraid of the toilet itself but is afraid of recurrence of bad experiences in the bathroom. Toilet training cannot proceed when this barrier is still present.

What to do:

You need to reestablish pleasant and positive feelings in your child about the potty or toilet. This includes:

1. Making use of stool softeners so that the feeling of bowel movements shifts from being painful to something that feels good and is pain free

2. Desensitize your child to using the toilet by giving a small reward such as candy or sweets. Desensitization can follow these six steps. The treat is ideally given once your child accomplishes each milestone.

Step 1: Your child or daughter empties her soiled diaper into the toilet bowl

Step 2: Your child passes stool or does a bowel movement into a diaper while inside the bathroom

Step 3: Your child passes stool or does a bowel movement into a diaper while sitting on the closed lid of a toilet

Step 4: Your child passes stool or does a bowel movement into a diaper while sitting on a toilet with the lid up

Step 5: Make use of a "magic diaper" or a diaper with a hole cut into it. Let your child pass stool or do a bowel movement through the magic diaper and into the toilet.

Step 6: Your child passes stool or does a bowel movement directly into the toilet without the help of a magic diaper.

Technique in case of Regression

It can happen that a potty-trained child can go back to the pre-potty training stage. There are several reasons for this. It could be due to a major life event that is causing a lot of stress or it could be a reaction change. The first thing is to make sure they are not suffering from any health-related problems and that their body systems are working fine. Reassure your child and avoid punishment as much as possible until you find out the root issue.

Chapter 15 - Additional Tips and Tricks for Potty Training

Not all potty training goes smoothly. Some children resist, preferring their diaper to the toilet. Some think the potty is toy. Some fight it every step of the way. Here is some advice on how to manage them if they rear up.

Starting Early

Some parents start addressing the issue with doctors at about 18 months, when they first start showing signs. Starting training at this age can be detrimental. You can purchase the potty chair and place it in the bathroom. Let them go in the bathroom when you and sit on it, but don't pressure them into go in the potty yet. Most toddlers aren't ready until at least 24 months. Give it time. It will happen.

Why did the Youngest Train Faster?

Families with more than one child will find that the youngest will train faster than a single child or the oldest child of the family. This is because there are more experienced potty users in the house, and this means there are more in the home to reinforce positive results.

Stools/Constipation

If you little one is having a hard time going, or says it hurts when he/she goes, A trip to the doctor may be warranted. Little ones get constipated as well. This leads to hard stools where it hurts for them to go. Some will have an uncomfortable look on their face as they go or look concerned before they go sit on the potty. Don't be afraid to ask them if they are having problems. You are guiding on this new phase of their life, and they need a lot of guidance.

To help avoid constipation, include some food high in fiber. If they intake about a thousand calories daily, 19 grams of fiber will keep them regular. Physical activity will also prevent constipation.

Reluctance to Go

They just refuse:

When toddlers learn the word "no", they like to use it, a lot. This includes telling you know when you ask if they have gone potty. Don't worry, and don't ask too frequently. Let them tell you or show you they have to go.

If they continue to refuse, and you are at home, place a potty chair in a centralized location and let them run around with no bottoms.

Ask them if they are afraid to use the potty. Some will express fear. Just talk to them and put them at ease.

Don't Hover

Don't make the process any harder than it has to be. If they don't go when you put them on the potty, don't make them sit there until something happens. This will cause a reluctance of using the potty.

When they have to go, don't hover over them and make sure they are going. Some toddlers will say they have to, sit on the potty, and nothing happens. This is normal. They are learning how to recognize the signs they have to go, and they not get it right all the time.

Having problems at day care

You may find out that your child is having problems going at her daycare. This may be due to the routine the day care employees in their potty-training policies. Many day care centers take children to the bathroom in groups, often making some of the younger ones that are training be too nervous to go. After all, you have been training her to go by herself, and now she has to go potty with others at the same time. There are two ways of handling this:

Talk to the day care employees. They may be able to modify the routine so that your little one will stop having problems.

In the meantime, when you're running errands, take him/her into a public potty and explain to them that it's perfectly normal to go potty with others. This will help them become comfortable going in public and when the day care employees take a group to the potty.

Has reverted to some degree

Routine is everything when you're potty training. If you change homes, day care, or even start going to the store on a different day may cause anxiety in the little one, making them revert to some degree. Children at this age are very sensitive to changes, problems, and marital strife, like arguing. All these things can make your little one reverts and wet themselves.

Start a reward system. Make a calendar and place a start on it whenever they go. Toys you think they will like and reward them with one when they go. Don't reward a successful potty run with food or sweets. This will cause problems in the future.

Won't Stop Playing to Go

This is a common problem with toddlers just starting their potty-training routine. The use of a timer or potty watch will let them know that it is time to stop what they are doing and go to the bathroom.

A potty watch is idea for a child who is still very active and does not stay in one place playing for a while.

A timer can be effective if the child sits in one place for a prolonged amount of time. When the timer goes off, politely remind them that it is time to go to the potty.

Plays with their poop

This may be somewhat disturbing to you, but they are still exploring their world. Don't yell at them if you see them do this. Calmly explain to them that the things that go in diapers, pull-ups, and the potty are not toys and they don't need to play with them.

There may also be an anxiety cause for this as well. If you suspect this is the case, again, go to your child's pediatrician. Let them know your concerns and they can help you get past this.

Wetting the bed

Some children wet the bed until they are in their teens, maybe once or twice a week. This is normal and may stem from being a heavy sleeper.

If they wet more than once or twice a week, there may be a deeper, both physical or psychological, issue and it needs to be addressed by a physician.

No more Diapers

Once you've upgraded to pull-ups or underwear, let your care giver know that you will no longer have needed them to put a diaper on your child. This will confuse him, making it more difficult to potty train her properly.

Tools for Training

There are a lot more product out there to help you train your child. Here are a few of the many.

Potty Chairs:

This is small little potty seat with a splash-proof rim. This is just the right size for a toddler to sit and use the potty. The bowl removes easily so you can put it in the toilet.

Potty Seat:

This is a seat that fits snuggly on the toilet, allowing the toddler to sit on the toilet to use it. Some have bowls so you can see if they went. These bowls are removable for disposal.

Step Stool:

This is a child-sized stool that can be placed at the toilet so they can climb up and use the toilet.

Buying all three can be a little pricey in the long run. There are products out there that convert into each of the three items above, so it grows when they do, following them at each stage.

Travel Potty:

If you travel a lot, this will be an indispensable training tool. It fits on any toilet and folds for travel. There are, any different types of travel potties on the market, so finding one that suits your needs and convenience shouldn't be a chore.

Pull-ups:

These are disposable training pants made by diaper companies to help with the training programs. They are designed to hold accidents and warn them when they need to go by allowing them to feel the moisture.

Training Pants:

If you want something that feels a little more like underwear, washable training pants will be what you are looking for to train your child. They come in many sizes, shapes, and styles.

Potty Dolls:

These training tools are to help your little better understand how to start their potty training. They come with an anatomically correct doll, a potty, and a reading material on potty training.

Potty Watches:

If you want your child to learn to stop what they're doing and potty on their own, you are going to need to pick up a potty wash. Depending on their potty habits, this watch can be set for thirty (30), sixty(60), and ninety(90) minutes. It is a countdown timer that lights up, and chimes to let the child know they need to go potty.

Potty Training Charts:

These charts are a complete rewards system for your little one. It contains stickers, charts, a reading material for training, and a keepsake certificate for when they are finished with their training. Once they have gotten three stickers on the chart, they get a reward, a toy, trip to the park, etc.

A Few More Tips and Tricks

There are a few things to remember when potty training that will make it easier for you and your wee one.

Don't pressure them

Even though they might show signs early, that doesn't mean it's time.

Don't sit them on the potty and don't let them off until they go.

This will make them be reluctant and not want to go.

It will cause them to hold it, and fight when it's time to go.

Don't reward them with sweet treats.

This will start a bad precedent and cause bad eating habits.

It will tie food to good actions, causing the child to do other things to get rewarded with treats of this nature.

Find what your little one likes the most, toys, reading materials with pictures, or other things that can be used for currency.

Come up with a little poop song.

We all have to poo. Make it fun to poop buy coming up with a song to help them push while they pass a stool.

Be observant.

Your little one will give you hints and cues.

Knowing when they have to go will help them to recognize when they have to go, making training easier and more effective.

Don't get mad at setbacks.

They will happen.

Handle each one with patience, grace, and understanding.

Let them know accidents happen and that it's alright.

Coordinate with your care givers

Make sure you are all on the same page when it comes to training your child.

This will insure your little one will always be comfortable going potty.

Make it a big deal when they go.

Congratulate them when they go on their own.

It will make them have a sense of pride.

It will make it easier to train them, wanting them to make you proud.

Don't shrug them off.

We're all busy, but we can't ever be too busy to pay attention when they are trying to tell us they have to go.

Keep in touch with your pediatrician

Let her know during check-ups how your little one is doing with her training.

Tell them your concerns if they are being reluctant or having problems going.

Work with your pediatrician to resolve behavioral issues to make the process smoother for you and your child.

Talk with other parents.

Other parents that have or are potty training may have ideas you haven't thought of to help train your little one.

Tell them your concerns and see what they have to say.

They have had to go through that with their little one.

Conclusion

Congratulations! You have made it to the finals, and I want to thank you for trusting us with this very crucial level to help your toddler. I want you to have a good start so that you will be successful in potty training. You have taken the necessary steps that many have not. You have taken the steps to get the data that will help you to achieve success.

Here are some last minutes tips for potty training your daughter in just three days.

Potty Training Day 1

Day 1 will constantly be the toughest.

But you simply have to be very effective and constantly lookout for your infant's use of her potty. The Potty should usually be in the restroom – It's better if the potty chair of your toddler is in the toilet so that she can just go there any time she wishes to use than, placing it in different regions of the house just like the lawn or dwelling room.

Always set the Training Tone of the Day – You ought to have a moderate approach when the training starts. You can use the naked-backside method in which you're going to apply real undies. Begin the day with a tale as you are taking off your baby's diaper while she wakes up. Explain to her what your intentions for the day are and, the way the potty chair could assist you in obtaining it.

Have Cleaning Tools Nearby – Potty education injuries are susceptible to take place so ensure that you have a bucket, a mop and a cleansing liquid close to you.

Potty Training Day 2

Day 2 will be an achievement for you if you practice the same approaches which you used on day 1. Let her be acquainted of the things you did on day 1. However, day two can be just like day 1. Don't be discouraged and just keep away from injuries to occur.

Potty Training Day 3

On day three, teach her that before she performs or does anything outside, she should pee first. If the 3-day potty schooling went on well, day three would surely be a pleasant surprise for you. If day three is already accident-free and your toddler has already acquainted or likely has mastered the right process, you do not need to move again on repeating the method you did on day 1 and 2.

Some Guidelines to help you know your baby is ready

1.) One thing to look at is, if your baby is eager to get your attention after they want to go to the bathroom.

2.) Another component is if your child already knows the way to put on and additionally get rid of their own underwear.

3.) Does your baby always want to use the restroom or are they curious about it?

4.) Does your toddler complain or sign to you that they have got soiled diapers?

5.) If your toddler is doing any of the above points, then it is a sure sign that they're in equipped for potty training.

1.) You will have to chat with your child and explain to them why you have to use the restroom. Most regularly than now, know-how is usually the key to achievement in every endeavor. Do not underestimate the functionality of your infant to understand. Science has indicated that toddlers have sharp memories and they may be maximally observed guidelines faster as compared to adults.

2.) Understanding can be faster and less difficult in case you display them visually. This is because youngsters are very visual. They tend to recognize extra if they have snapshots. Show your child pix with directions and instructions for potty training. You ought to additionally introduce them to the restroom. Instruct them how it's been done. Teach them a way to sit on the bowl and flush it. Flushing the bowl additionally excites toddlers.

The cool flushing sound makes them extra interested.

3.) Letting them wear diapers will truly slow their training. If they do not wear diapers and/or underclothes, they will look for an area to poo and/or pee.

During their sleep, do not allow them to wear diapers. Most frequently, they may wet the bed. This is the proper time to hold them and cause them to do it in the restroom. This can be a sacrifice on your side due to the fact that you additionally ought to awaken and accompany them. However, it is going to be worth it. This step is merely the most effective way to train them.

4.) Every time they do the training proper, praise them. Children stay up for rewards. Appreciate them very well. They want to be praised all of the time. Doing this can make them to do it properly in the future.

If you are a busy mom and want to potty train fast, comply with the steps above.

You'll get the process performed in less than a week. I hope those potty-training recommendations will assist. When you have got fulfillment on the potty, provide a HUGE reward. Lots of clapping; high fives; you did it! I'm so pleased with you! and so on. Give them lots of verbal praise and, give them a reward that they're stimulated to have. It's truly crucial that the reward is specific to what they want and are truly interested in.

Example: Don't deliver stickers if they don't care for stickers. For my daughter, it was placing up pictures of favorite cartoon characters on her wall; it simply needs to be unique to what your kid enjoys. You want them to be stimulated to reap the reward.

How to motivate your Child for Potty training

A lot of information out there will inform you that to inspire your baby, you need to visit the shop and select up a toy or something like that.

Though that's good, I'll give you something even better when it comes to motivation.

Here's the trouble with giving them toys or telling them, "I'm taking your toys away," and in reality, you're taking the toy away and hiding it, so they don't see it. When children are among the ages of 2 and 5, out of sight means out of thoughts, the average interest span at that age is about 7 minutes.

So, that motivation does not go a long way. What I love to do is use fear of gain vs. fear of loss. Now, let me explain the distinction to you among fear of gain and fear of loss. Most human beings even as adults consider it nowadays. Fear of loss is a larger motivator than fear of gain. You may be announcing this; "If you behave, you may get…" or, "If you use the potty, you may get…" Although it may be a very good component for

motivation, I think you can get a higher reaction through announcing,

"If you don't use the potty, you may lose this." In other words, if they don't use the potty, they're going to lose something.

Let me come up with an instance of one of the motivations we used to use with my first daughter. We needed to "outsmart the fox" as I call it. I used to mention somethings like, "Dana, do you need to go to McDonald's?" And he'd say, "Yes, let's visit McDonald's."

So, then I would say, "Okay, super! Go get your coat. Go get your shoes. Let's go to McDonald's." She'd go get her stuff, and we'd open the front door and get ready to stroll out. And then I would say, "Oh, you know what Dana, Let's use the toilet before we pass because you don't want to have a coincidence at Ronald McDonald's residence." So, what did I do it at that time? Using fear of loss, I defuse the potty.

At that time, dropping McDonald's became way more vital to her than the restroom. So, she went without any problem.

Now, going this McDonald's way, you need to spend cash, but there are other ways that you could use this identical methodology inside your residence. For example, you could use their favored cookie or their favorite snack.

Let's say they like pudding. You would possibly say, "Hey Dana, do you need a few puddings?" And the answer, of course, is going to be, "Yes." You then take the pudding, you placed it on the desk, and you position the spoon in the bowl, you absolutely let them snatch the spoon; get geared up to take a bite and then you say, "Wait for a second. Before you're taking that chunk, let's use the potty."

At this time, the pudding and the praise are so important to the kid that the potty is not anything again for him. They'll use the potty so they could return and get that reward. You can do that with the toys as well.

You also can do it on TV. If it's a television program that they like, then I might wait till the show is about to start and I'd say, "Hey, let's use the toilet before we start watching the show." If they say, "Oh the display is starting; I don't want to use the restroom." Then, your answer is, "Let's go quick if you want to watch that display. "Until we use the restroom, the display isn't going to be on." Then, you could actually turn the TV off. So, that is the manner to inspire them. You don't need to use the normal phrase, "I'm taking the toys away."

Remember, you want to be steady.

Consistency is one of the most vital things that you may do right now to your kid to assist them in potty training. If there is something which you learn from us all this while, please let that be that consistency is vital.

Secondly is the 'push.' Every time your child sits on that toilet, ensure they're pushing the potty. Once they push, they can get up even when they've not done anything in the restroom.

Remember you're the prize. You are the figure, and you need to set how the training will go.

You're pulling strings, so remember that as your child is looking to push the bounds, you have got to be set. As a human, this method can be frustrating. This method may be hard, and we take into account that, and so we're telling you to be a parent.

You're going to be pissed off, you're going to be mad, and you may even yell a million times. But don't let that discourage you.

Be happy and genuine to yourself.

Most importantly, as we said, get some relaxation due to the fact you'll be stressed for the duration of this training process. We wish you good luck and lots of laughs. Be strong!

Made in the USA
Middletown, DE
16 October 2020